HURON COUNTY LIBRARY

3 6492 00522077 4

D1173840

796.86092 MacKa

MacKay, S.
Running with swords.

PRICE: $27.95 (3559/cl)

Running With Swords

Running With Swords

*The Adventures and Misadventures of
the Irrepressible Canadian Fencing Champion*

Sherraine MacKay

Fitzhenry & Whiteside

Running With Swords
Copyright © 2005 Sherraine MacKay

All rights reserved. No part of this book may be reproduced in any manner without the express written consent of the publisher, except in the case of brief excerpts in critical reviews and articles. All inquiries should be addressed to:

Fitzhenry and Whiteside Limited
195 Allstate Parkway, Markham, Ontario L3R 4T8

In the United States:
311 Washington Street, Brighton, Massachusetts, 02135

www.fitzhenry.ca godwit@fitzhenry.ca

Fitzhenry & Whiteside acknowledges with thanks the Canada Council for the Arts, and the Ontario Arts Council for their support of our publishing program. We acknowledge the financial support of the Government of Canada through the Book Publishing Industry Development Program (BPIDP) for our publishing activities.

ONTARIO ARTS COUNCIL
CONSEIL DES ARTS DE L'ONTARIO

Canada Council Conseil des Arts
for the Arts du Canada

Library and Archives Canada Cataloguing in Publication

MacKay, Sherraine
Running with swords : the adventures and misadventures of the irrepressible
Canadian fencing champion / Sherraine MacKay.

ISBN 1-55041-982-X
1. MacKay, Sherraine. 2. Women fencers—Canada—Biography. I. Title.
GV1144.2.M35A3 2005   796.86'092   C2005-902887-4

United States Cataloguing-in-Publication Data

MacKay, Sherraine.
Running with swords : the adventures and misadventures of the irrepressible Canadian fencing
champion / Sherraine MacKay
[256] p. : photos. ; cm.
Summary : An autobiography of Olympic Fencing Athlete Sherraine MacKay.
ISBN 1-55041-982-X (pbk.)
1. MacKay, Sherraine. 2. Fencing – Canada. I. Title.
796.8/6 /0922 [B] dc22   GV1144.2.M35 2005

Cover design by Kerry Designs
Cover image courtesy of Peter Bregg
Backcover image courtesy of Peter Bregg
Interior design by Karen Petherick, Intuitive Designs International Ltd.
Insert images: page ii, courtesy of Oswald Schalm; pages iii, iv, v, vi (bottom image),
and vii courtesy of Peter Bregg; page vi (top image) courtesy of Jeff Shantz
Printed and bound in Canada

1 3 5 7 9 10 8 6 4 2

To my parents who raised me to be myself and be it well.

And to Geordie who loves me for myself and loves me well.

Contents

Introduction

A man has control over many things in his life;
he has control over enough things to be the
hero of a novel. But if he had control over
everything, there would be so much hero that
there would be no novel ... The thing which
keeps life romantic and full of fiery possibilities is
the existence of these great plain limitations
which force all of us to meet the things we do
not like or do not expect.

— G. K. Chesterton

A ll the pieces had fallen into place. I'd learned to enter a still state of being, a numb awareness in which my movements came from my mind, body and instincts. That intensity is a force to be reckoned with and on May 21st 2000 in Seville, Spain, the rest of the fencing world had to reckon with my sword. This was the day I made history for Canadian fencing: I became the first Canadian woman to win a World Cup. Being the best, even if only once, made me feel like I belonged, and all those days spent wondering, "will it ever be me," well, that question was suddenly answered. It was me *today*. I was no longer just Sherraine Schalm from Brooks, Alberta, who enjoys fencing; I could now call myself a *world-class fencer* with no twinge of doubt.

The whole day felt like it was moving in slow motion as I kept advancing, winning round after round until I was in the final up against Claudia Bokel, a German girl I had grown up admiring as she dominated the junior circuit and quickly did the same in the senior. As usual, I didn't have a coach with me so Julie Leprohon, the only other Canadian girl in attendance, stepped in to fill the role of official advice-giver. "You're doing well, keep moving and being smart and you should keep winning" was the beautifully simplistic line I remember.

Our match was tight and it went right to the last few seconds as Claudia rushed at me to even up the score. I didn't want sudden-death overtime with such an experienced fencer so I tried to avoid her attacks until time ran out. *"3 – 2 – 1- Halt!"* I had won a World Cup! As I took off my mask, I tried to fully absorb the feeling of pure excellence that was washing over me. I had not lost an entire match all day! Claudia and I shook hands and suddenly I was overwhelmed that I was even on the same podium piste with a childhood idol, never mind that I had beaten her.

At last I was going to hear my national anthem! I could cry like Catriona Le May Doan or sing like Ross Rebagliati. I stood waiting on the highest platform of the podium, straining to hear the first few bars of the song we all know from every weekday in school and every weekend on *Hockey Night in Canada*.

After some uncomfortable silence, the crowd started to get restless but finally there was a click over the speaker system as the music started. It took a few seconds to register that what I was hearing was not the wistful horns of "O Canada" but the energetic guitars and castanets of salsa music. I looked over at the organizers with a furrowed brow. They shrugged their shoulders and motioned toward a box containing cassettes of several national anthems. They hadn't even considered bringing a recording of Canada's national anthem. I guess I was a surprise champion.

THE GREAT REPRESSION

E very good story has a beginning and, at the risk of sounding absurd, my Olympic journey could be traced back to my grandparents, Adolf and Emilie Schalm. They were Germans who had lived in Poland until immigrating to Canada for reasons of risky nomenclature; that, and because they were homeless. They moved to northern Saskatchewan in 1927 to take advantage of the Canadian government's generous promise of free land. Those of you who have travelled throughout Europe know that land is hard to come by in the old country. If you do manage to acquire some, say, by inheritance, a duel or offering your firstborn son into the priesthood, you could set yourself and your family up. Failing this, you could do as our Canadian forefathers did and adopt a country in which coming into some property didn't entail family feuds, pistols at dawn or bitter inductees into the clergy. Some of our forefathers knew what they might be getting into, that there were entire provinces so full of mosquitoes and thorn bushes that they were almost uninhabitable. One such place was Saskatchewan. Only true refugees would want to live there. The government folks decided to offer "Free Saskatchewan Farmland," which showed that they were the same type of people who give their old nursing uniforms and teething toys to the Salvation Army under the reasoning, "if it's free, *somebody's* gonna use it." Imagine Adolf and Emilie's shock, after travelling 15,000 kilometres on ship, coach, boxcar and foot with their three strapping children, to see their Canadian gift: a pile of rocks laced with scabby trees, theirs to share with a diverse community of New World insects.

I can just imagine my grandfather reaching down to slap a mosquito that had taken a vicious bite out of his thigh as he assessed his new property: "Vell, it's not my vishful vegetable garden beside the Rhine, and Emilie," he said as he looked with a raised eyebrow at his three children, one of whom was madly whacking every surface of his own body to prevent further blood loss as the other two tried to keep from being airlifted by bugs to the next village, "ve are not yet in best condition to be real farm …"

My Grandma, who correctly understood that as German for "I want you, I need you," set her face resolutely, and they subsequently had seven more children, determined to eke out a living for them all.

My father was one of those 10 little settlers born into poverty. He entered the world screaming and crying, but not on account of the doctor spanking him, because, well, there *was* no doctor. My dad was helped into the world under a sod-roofed house by some childless woman in the neighbourhood, Mrs. Sweirs (pronounced "Swears"), who probably became a de facto midwife in response to the curses of the local women in labour.

If childbirth wasn't challenging enough for my grandparents, there was the follow-up of having to raise their 10 kids. This meant hand-washing clothes on a scrub board, growing all their own food as well as a surplus of crops to sell, and cooking for at least twelve people three times per day, every day. Adolf used whatever free time he had left to learn English because he happened to also be the community pastor.

Needless to say, in this harsh environment people were too

busy with daily survival to pay attention to frivolities such as sports. Everyone, that is, except my dad, Oswald.

While I don't think my grandpa went as far as to say, "Sports are from the devil," this was the general attitude of pastors and farmers in the northern Saskatchewan community. Seeing as my grandfather was both, Oswald had a hard sell on his hands. Adolf was no dummy, however, and he knew how to motivate people. The way my dad would reward us with all the change on his dresser or an extra hour of television, Adolf would let Oswald participate in sports-oriented projects. One day (Dad must have rescued a child from a well or single-handedly stopped a prairie fire) Adolf let him use the extra wood from clearing farmland to make his own wooden skis. That episode, along with organizing a church softball game and his acquisition of the only set of boxing gloves in the community, had my dad considering himself sort of a founding father of a sports system that was both extremely amateur and nightmarishly competitive.

Adolf drew the line at professional sports, however, and forbade his children to tune the family radio to those vile Saturday night hockey games. Saturday night was for praying and knitting. So the boys would wait until Adolf had sat down to do his evening knitting (his socks were his glory) and then they would secretly run their homemade speaker extension into the kitchen, silently cheering when they heard the tinny, "He shoots, he scores!" If they were ever caught while listening late in the game, there was a good chance they were praying (for the Leafs), so they probably escaped the switch often enough to embolden them. Having so many brothers and sisters probably also helped my dad: he only had to soak up a share of the punishment. And there was always one of them furtively standing guard to report the creaking of the floorboards under Grandpa's chair as he rose to check on them.

These years of repression ended when my father went away to teachers' college at age 17, and saw his first gymnasium. He realized that sports were more than a reward for hauling stones at daybreak. Away from the disapproving eye of Grandpa, my dad could finally play sports with reckless abandon. He made sure all of his kids played every sport available.

Many years later—thankfully, after Mrs. Sweirs had retired—another screaming child was brought (well, more like forced) into the world. My parents met in teachers' college, fell in love, got married and decided to change their scenery from dry, flat, insect-ridden northern Saskatchewan to dry, flat, insect-ridden Brooks, Alberta. They considered this the big move to civilization. In keeping with this, I was born in a hospital, and how much the better for it! I was the last of my mother's five children and, so it seemed, the ugly duckling. I popped out looking like a human percussion set, with a clubfoot and a clicking hip (I was born with what is called developmental dysplasia of the hip). People who see the cup as half empty walked by the incubator and said to my shocked mother, "Well, hopefully she'll end up being smart …" Cup-half-fulls might have said, "Well praise the Lord—with those wonky legs and skewed hips your baby has a natural stance for fencing and should probably become a top Olympian!"

Determination is a standard Olympic trait, and if I inherited it from anyone, it was from my mother, Liz. As if having four other children wasn't enough work, her fifth would require constant care as an infant. For my first three weeks of life I remained in the hospital; my mother walked from their tiny apartment every three hours to feed me as I lay like a soft, pink pretzel in my hospital bed. She finally brought me home with my gifts of corrective ankle weights and leg pulleys. My older sister Jonene was excited to see that this new baby came with toys! After receiving explicit threats of punishment for any sort of playing on or around me, Jonene left me alone. "Even though your younger sister's strings and pulleys look perfect for playing the harp, cat's cradle, or G.I. Joe mountaineer, you are NOT to touch her." So now I was a handful *and* a curiosity.

In keeping with the ugly duckling theme, the corrective devices that made me look like a modern art display would serve a grander plan when I was older. God was not only restoring me with those chains, he was giving me an edge! What other baby have you ever seen lifting weights while the rest were chewing on soothers or cuddling dolls? I was in heavy training before I was in training pants. My mom knew that this would put me ahead, so she felt no need to encourage me to crawl, walk or even sit up. "Oh, Doctor Worms said she would be just fine after this treatment. Soon she'll be running around like the rest of the kids," Mom would say a little too confidently to visitors, and a little less confidently to herself when she was alone changing my diaper.

None of this bothered me; I knew under all the binder twine and rusted steel I was a swan. I just sat it out patiently tied up to my crib weight machine for the first 11 months of my life, catching my breath in between sets. I was released just before my first birthday, and I skipped the crawling and started walking—straight as an arrow. This shocked everyone except my mother and Doctor Worms. I guess if you're a mom you always have faith, and if you grew up with the last name Worms, you have learned to ignore the doubtful whispers of others. But don't worry, I never forgot my roots. Late at night when my mom would come in to confirm that I hadn't manifested any more genetic malfunctions, my feet would be at right angles assuming the *en guard* position, only this time without the click and the club foot.

When my parents talk about what I was like growing up, the words "determined" and "funny" come up over and over. You need both of these traits if, like me, you picked the "Endurance Run" as your event for the Canada Fitness tests in grade school. I was never a good runner, and as usual I came in dead last. But as my dad tells the story, this in no way diminished my spirit. Apparently, as I was running along, I was wasting my precious breath *singing* (some Beatles tune, no doubt) as I went down the track. My dad watched me heading down the home stretch, singing and trotting merrily and he thought, "I gotta get a picture of this!" I guess I didn't notice the fact that everyone else had finished ahead of me. Brightening even more at the sight of a camera lens, I flashed my dad a smile and gave him an "I'm number one!" sign as I went by. The shutter clicked and I kept on singing right to the finish line.

No one would have said that I was extremely well behaved, but I was never intentionally bad. This was not out of respect for anyone in particular, but just out of good old-fashioned fear of authority figures. Rather than blatantly breaking rules I would try to charm people into giving me what I wanted, mostly using my weird sense humour and motor mouth. I didn't know when to shut up, so I got in a lot of trouble chatting my way through classes, sports, music or church—but never anything serious. Anyone who fell into serious trouble in my hometown was either avoided or sent off to live somewhere else; in our innocence we assumed that big trouble only happened in the "big city."

Brooks was anything but a typical town to grown up in. Its highlights are permanent rodeo grounds, a cow slaughtering plant and a mall with "25 Stores to Serve You Better." For a town like Brooks, what was even stranger was the existence of a fencing club. Sure, it was a prairie town with your usual bovines, farmers and misled Western separatists, but there was a weirder sort of folk who refused to listen to country music and instead partic-ipated in odd, Quebecer-type sports like … fencing. Ironically enough, the club was not started by a French-speaking Canadian, but an ex-pat Englishman, Alan Nelson, who moved, via Toronto, to the prairies in 1981 to log a few years of teaching experience. In the meantime, he started up a local fencing club to install some English-style recreation in the community. I guess it worked, because 23 years later he is still at the same school running the same fencing club. Besides Germany, the land of my grandparents, my Olympic dream in a way could be traced back to the windy shores of Liverpool, the hometown of Alan's parents, who first immigrated to Canada in 1967.

Alan was the coolest teacher in town. He was the only one who listened to the same music that we did, with the notable exception of the New Kids on the Block. He wore the same clothes that we did, with the obvious exception of a training bra; and he had the same enthusiasm and energy that we did, only his didn't come from downing three Slurpees at lunchtime. When I saw him, I knew I had to be around him.

Unfortunately, I was an 11-year-old cheeky monkey who mistook being a smart aleck for having charisma. One day after school, just as he was getting into his car, I yelled out in my most desperate I-am-the-youngest-of-five-children-so-please-notice-me voice, "Hey, Skinny!" I waited for him to turn around and notice me. When he whipped around to slap a detention on the kid who had just yelled the insult, he realized I'd yelled it at him. In the uncomfortable pause that followed, I walked over to continue our "conversation." My mature side told me that the best way to get this teacher to like me was to show him that I know something about him, so I blurted out, "Hey, I hear you have a fencing club!"

"Yes, that's true," he said, startled. His voice trailed off and he just looked at me oddly.

"So can I join?"

Searching for a polite way to say no to this living mouth-on-legs, Alan asked, "Well, let's see, how old are you?"

Unsure what age would make him like me more, I hesitated but finally decided to go with the truth, a decision I would later regret. "Eleven."

"There you go!" he breathed easy, "You have to be at least junior-high age to join."

I couldn't believe his gall! Here I was, willing to join his stupid fencing club, and he wasn't going to let me because I hadn't lived long enough? I decided to pull rank. My eyebrows rose suggestively, "But ... my dad's your boss ..."

"I don't care!" he retorted, and opened his car door and stepped in. "I'll see you in a year!"

Walking away from that conversation I was thinking two things: that guy sure doesn't take any guff, and, boy am I going to get it when my mom hears what I said to a teacher!

When the next year came around, I was so eager to start fencing that I almost didn't notice how much I hated it.

"Hey, Skinny!"

Growing up, individual sports were never really my thing. If child psychologists had had the pleasure of studying my behaviour in the schoolyard, they might have assessed me thus: left-brain attention seeker on a sugar high. By the time I was eight, my mother had spent many hours listening as my coaches and teachers tried to delicately tell her that I was displaying some—*ahem*—abnormal behaviour. These problems rarely arose out of anger, impatience or spite, but mostly out of pure weirdness. Before long, I was trying one sport after another, my individualist streak always coming through.

Like most Canadian children at that time, I just had to try figure skating. Figure skating was worrisome for my parents, not just because it cost a lot of money, but because if I wasn't very good at it I could fall and really hurt myself. In the end, the falling wasn't as much a problem as the getting up. I would just lie giggling on the ice oblivious to the frostbite spreading up my skinny butt. "Pretty please, Sherraine, get up now. We have to practice the Walt Disney routine one more time before the recital or Mickey will get *really* upset and have to pay a visit to your *mother* ..."

Oh, come on, honey. I might be six years old, but who actually thinks that Mickey is going to fly all the way from California to meet with my mom, no matter how disappointed he is in my toe-loop. When my instructors would try to pull me up, I would go limp and chant: "I'm a corpse! I'm a corpse!" Another meeting for Mom, and time to find another sport.

The ice had melted, the weather was warming, so baseball seemed to make sense. To avoid multiple trips into town (a 10-minute commute is unthinkable in Brooks) I was put on the same team as my older sister Jonene; Dad was coaching. Forget my figure-skating corpse routine, this time the parent-instructor interview would become the parents-child discipline session if I didn't grow up a little

He wanted me to love it, truly he did, but for my dad, loving a sport meant mastering it, which clearly I did not do. After the first practice, my dad decided I needed extra training because unlike my nearly perfect sister, I threw "improperly" for a seven-year-old. You can't doubt the old man's enthusiasm. Despite being almost fanatical, his fervour did nothing to improve my baseball skills. We spent hours in the backyard, only the pulsating veins in his temple betraying his frustration as I tried in vain to drop my shoulder, lead with the elbow and flick my wrist on the follow-through at least *once* before the sun went down. Jonene came along to help, and I could see her wanting me to succeed for all of our sakes. My dad would crouch, waiting for me to throw him the ball.

"Okay now, Sherraine, just take the ball and lean back with your right foot ... no, your *right* foot. Jonene can you just run over there and show her the right foot? Okay now, step forward with your left foot ... left. Jonene, again, please? Now drop your shoulder. No, not the ball, pick that up again. Let your *shoulder* drop. Good. And now lead with your elbow ... Jonene, can you just guide her elbow a bit? Thanks, sweetheart. Now flick your wrist and let the ball go!"

The ball landed with a thud about two feet in front of me. I had thrown it vertically, so unless our team was challenging the Smurfs, I was no asset. Oswald was not to be defeated, however.

"Okay then, we'll work on catching … Jonene can you toss me the ball, please?" I watched in crushing envy as my sister casually took the ball and with a gentle, accurate inside curve, threw it flawlessly into my dad's mitt. "Thanks," he said, as I watched unconcealed admiration pass over his face. In no time, however, he gathered up his wits and remembered why we had spent the whole evening in the backyard. "Sherraine, you're up! Catching practice!"

I resigned myself to the fact that some things cannot be bred and that baseball was just not my bag. Somewhere behind his refusal to accept my lack of athleticism, my father must have agreed because during the next practice, while he was out there teaching my sister and the other 10-year-olds how to slide and dive into base, he sent me to run around the outfield. During the games, my role was more problematic because I actually had to play, so they put me in the esteemed position of left field. Don't go feeling sorry for me: almost forgotten about, I was free to run around and catch butterflies with my glove! If we lost, I didn't really notice because I was too far from the action to hear the groans of disappointment. If we won, I was still included in the victory visit to 7-Eleven for Slurpees! Baseball wasn't too bad after all, and I guess if I had to participate in something, team sports were the thing for me.

As I grew older, I realized that growing up in a small town meant that most decisions were made for me. One decision made without my approval was that I would do *all* of the same sports and hobbies that *all* of my older siblings had done, combined. When you are the youngest of five, this puts a lot on your plate. This meant that I "chose" to swim; skate; join the Pioneer Girls; play the piano, trumpet and accordion; play volleyball, basketball, baseball; and do track or field. Being my parents' youngest child meant that there wasn't any pressure on me to succeed at those activities but I was constantly running from school to sport to hobby with barely enough time to change my clothes. Basketball practice was at 6:45 in the morning; fencing practice was after school. I went to piano lessons in the royal blue polyester skirt that was my Pioneer Girls uniform so there would still be time to grab a quick bite at the Dairy Queen in between it all. When I was given more freedom, it was easy. In typical younger sibling fashion, I wanted to do whatever big sister Jonene was doing.

I tried out for the basketball and volleyball teams when I entered Grade 7 at age 12, all the while following Jonene. While she was immediately put on the senior teams for both sports, they put me on the junior team because I was way too tall to cut from the team, but too gangly and uncoordinated to play with the senior team. To this day I have no idea why, but somebody filmed one of our junior basketball games. Our coach, Mrs. Powell, provided a yelling commentary of advice and encouragement that went like this: "Okay girls, down the court now. Remember, you have to bounce the ball when you run with it ... okay on defence, then— Sherraine, you can't slap her arm, just the ball ... Now get the ball! ... Okay, good! Pass it! ... No, not to their players ..." In spite of a discouraging beginning, Mrs. Powell bore with us and we had such fun as a team that I ended up loving basketball. I would later convince my basketball teammates to come and join fencing in an attempt to make that sport bearable.

You see, right at the beginning of Grade 7 I had done as threatened and joined the fencing team. After a few weeks, however, I realized it wasn't all swashbuckling and swinging from the chandeliers. There was a lot to learn, a lot to pay attention to, and the tiniest fraction of a mistake could cost you! Above all, it was focus, focus, focus. Not easy for a kid in Grade 7, especially one who not so long ago had enjoyed playing ice-corpse.

Now in Brooks, Alberta, fencing was never thought to be done with swords. If there was no mention of barbed wire, people didn't know what in tarnation you were talking about. So I have invented many descriptions to relate what it feels like to do a sport while holding a sword. Although swords (épées) may all look the same, once you begin to understand the sport you realize that épées are very personal items. Think about it as a pair of shoes. You may wear the same size as someone else but when you put them on you know right away whether they are a good fit or not. If they aren't, you don't feel like you can do a thing in them. It is the same with épées. You know just how much angle, flexibility and curve your épée needs before you can comfortably fence. Worse comes to worse (like the airlines losing your fencing bag before a World Cup competition), you can use someone else's on the circuit but it is never the same as your own.

First off, the épée: it is just a bit heavier than a bottle of Coke but the weight is distributed over one metre which makes precision more difficult than you might imagine. Since I use a "French grip" it is basically a straight handle that gives me some extra inches on the back end of my sword. This is a great addition making my unnaturally long arms even longer but it sort of "front loads" my épée, making it feel heavier and more awkward than the ortho-pedic or "pistol" grip. The blade itself is bent slightly, curving downward to help it feel balanced and natural in your hand.

The uniform (although modified for safety of course—now it is extremely safe and can withstand broken épées and helps disperse the impact of being hit) looks relatively similar to the old-fash-ioned white uniforms of yore with the traditional wire-mesh masks, unadorned besides your name and small national emblem. Fencing is quite similar to tennis at Wimbledon where European institutions maintain the traditions that have "served so properly" in the past. In fact, our sport almost had its own anti-establishment Andre Agassi type when Italian World Champion Paolo Milanoli painted a vicious clown face on his mask for the 2001 World Championships in Nimes, France. Paolo wore it successfully, glow-ering at everyone through pointed teeth and a big red nose until the televised final when the International Fencing Federation decided enough was enough and he would have to behave like everyone else. Understanding the Federation's point of view and because he wanted to be allowed to continue in the competition, he donned a regular black one. His clown mask he coyly placed at the end of the piste and during the intermission he would consult it instead of his coach. The fact that he became World Champion that day might say something about the need for personal expression—or maybe that clown just gave really good advice.

We wear a long-sleeve jacket along with an extra protective half-jacket underneath that goes on your fencing arm and shoulder. Our pants go only to the knees because our sport involves a lot of lunging action. Not to expose any flesh (obviously because the other person is wielding a sword) we wear long socks, and the smart ones among us wear a shin guard. Before the competition begins the uniform weighs about two and a quarter kilograms, and the mask is about 1 kilogram. Soaking with sweat at the end of the day, you can easily add another full kilo.

With all this protective equipment, getting poked is really not a big deal. Remember, we train for agility and subtlety of movement, not brute force and ignorance. It is all done fairly quickly: you are moving forward and backward and your body is always poised and ready to hit and be hit. It is usually unsurprising which almost always makes it hurt less. There are a few times when it really hurts, usually when it hits bone (shin—hence the shin guards—collar bone, hip or kneecap), or the fingers, but otherwise your body has enough adrenaline pumping through it that you are ready for the poke. Imagine someone takes one of those spring-loaded ballpoint pens: the kind that you have to click on and off. Then they reach out and jab you with the clicking part. The uncomfortable pressure you feel is about what it feels like to get poked with an épée. Of course I have to put a disclaimer on this description: it depends who you are fencing against! There are some people who have no sense of distance and hit you hard when you are fairly close. There are some who have no sense of timing and hit you after you have already hit them. Then there are people who are very good at distance and timing but they just hit hard. Recently, at a training camp in Hungary, Gabor Boczko, Olympic team medallist and one of the top guys in the world, asked me to fence. There are certain men I can fence well but they don't look like him:

over six feet and more than 200 pounds of pure aggression. So we started to fence. My style did not challenge him at all so I felt I needed to try harder physically. At one moment, he took a step forward as I did a running attack into him. The tip of his épée landed directly and excruciatingly in the crook of my arm. I was in so much pain that everything went white. Then I looked at my arm and I guess the initial shock must have subsided because soon I saw more than white—in fact I saw red. Blood was seeping from my new wound through my jacket. I tried to keep going because I didn't want to look weak. But Gabor stopped the match and said, "Yes you are very strong now, let's get someone to look at that." Since fencing has a tradition of chivalry, later that night he gave me a nice bottle of wine as an "elixir to make the pain go away."

Otherwise, painful encounters in fencing are fairly uncommon.

The actual fencing event takes place on a "piste" which is a metal surface 14-metres long and 2-metres wide. While our uniforms are still traditional looking, the scoring is now deter-mined through an electronic box that registers a hit with a colour-coded light. In épée, everything on the whole person is a target so our swords register a point as soon as the spring-loaded tip of the épée is depressed beyond 750 grams of pressure. This pressure closes an electrical circuit with the wire glued along the length of the blade which connects to a cord that is placed inside the fencer's jacket and hooked up to a retractable reel at the end of the piste. To debunk some common myths, the electric cord is not to hold the fencers back from charging at each other, it merely conducts electricity to register who hit who. Ah, and that elec-tricity does not give anyone an electric shock. Ever. The piste is metallic so that it can be ground out and prevent the electric scoring device from registering a hit when you touch the floor, hopefully keeping everything fair and square.

So in Brooks I started by learning the proper stance, then grad-uated to stepping forward and backward, "balestra," which is a sort of noisy hop meant to intimidate; lunging; and my favourite, the "flèche." Flèche means arrow in French, and that is certainly the best way to describe this move—a fast attack in which you push on your front leg, shoot your back leg forward and almost leap straight for your opponent, with an aim to actually hit her with your sword *before* your feet touch the ground. It probably comes as no surprise that Mr. Nelson, his thin body not unlike an actual arrow, had one of the best flèches in the world and he worked tirelessly to pass it on to me. It would take a long time to learn how to flèche properly, and of course at that point I had no idea that my future would hold high-level athletic performance, but the flèche would certainly do me good in those years to come.

And that's just the footwork! My brain was dazzled by the amount of actual "sword play" there was in fencing. Attack, remise. Taking of the blade, ripostes. Parry prime, seconde, quarte, sixte, septime or octave. Preparation, counter-attack, and renewal of attack. Phew!

Not to mention the rules. Fencing is a sport in which the rules descend from notions of actual fair play, honour, and respect. I was to not only salute my opponent with a raised sword at the beginning of a match—I was to salute again at the end, and shake hands, and salute the referee! If my opponent was to turn her back on me (a no-no), I should *not* take advantage of the fact and whack her for the impropriety. If she stumbled and fell, I should stop immediately, and even offer to help her to her feet. I was not to act out, yell inappropriately, pout, argue, or whine. I should take my hits as well as I should give them. And I should *never ever* run with my sword. All jokes aside, in this case it was true—I could put someone's eye out!

There was actual work to be done in order to improve, and the consequences of underperformance were painful: you got hit! In basketball, if you missed a shot the worst that could happen was that you had to run back down the court and play defence. If you missed in fencing, your opponent could smack you with a steel sword in all sorts of tender areas. (Don't worry, the "sensitive" zones are well protected with plastic or metal cups.) While I'm thankful for my equipment nowadays, for a skinny, underdeveloped

12-year-old kid, equipment could be a nightmare in itself. Since Mr. Nelson's charm extended to almost every kid in school, sooner or later everyone from the music geeks to the hockey jocks all came out to try fencing. Near the beginning, when I almost quit out of despair and exhaustion while learning to fence, my big crush at the time, Jason, joined the club. Of course now I *couldn't* quit fencing because the most popular hockey player was committed to spending every Thursday after school sparring with me.

Although my crush started off with the burning passion that only a teenage girl can experience, it soon faded as Jason "The Fox" found a way to humiliate me in the way only a teenage boy can. We had suited up to fence each other, and because we were fencing foil, we had to test to make sure that our electric jackets were functioning properly, so they would record a hit when one was made. To do this, you need to touch the tip of your foil anywhere on the metallic surface of the other person's jacket. There was no rule stating that we were required to aim directly for the bosom, or in my case, where a bosom would most likely be located in a few years. However, Jason put all his youthful energy behind the test hit. He aimed straight at my boob and poked. He was almost more surprised than I when a hollow "tock" sound resonated throughout the gym.

In a second he had burst out laughing and called his buddies over to catch "Act Two" of *Sherraine's Impossibly Small Chest*.

"Hey guys! Check this out! Her boob cups are hollow, there's nothing there! Sherraine's got no boobs!" Just Jason yelling "boobs!" was shocking enough to me, never mind that he was drawing attention to their size! I had already been accused of making Corey Hart look like he had a pimple on his forehead when I wore my *Fields of Fire* T-shirt. I didn't need this to confirm what I already knew: I was behind schedule. To my horror, Jason proceeded to chase me around the gym, stabbing at my chest as I ducked and weaved my way to where Mr. Nelson was. Thankfully, Mr. Nelson cut in yelling something about never running with a sword, and the scene grinded to a halt, but the emotional damage was already done and I disliked fencing even more.

As the year went on, fencing wasn't getting to be any more fun, but good old-fashioned fear of my dad made me stick with it. Every Thursday, all year long, I would grudgingly go off to my two-hour practice. But at the end of the year, Mr. Nelson rewarded those of us who had stuck with the sport with what for me would be a turning point. He entered us in a provincial competition! We piled into a van and drove up to Calgary. Once there, we entered a gym that could have been like any other, except this one was full to the brim with "pistes" (metal fencing strips, where the actual fencing took place), fencers, coaches, and referees. I was immediately part of a pool of girls all ready to fence their way into the elimination rounds. The gym soon filled with the noise of clashing weapons, ringing scoring machines, and shouts of triumph. I found myself incredibly excited simply at the prospect of challenging someone I didn't know.

It was at that first competition when I was 12 that I realized why we had spent all year doing footwork and practicing moves to perfection: so we could outmanoeuvre our big-city opponents. By the end of the day it was irrelevant to me that I had outmanoeuvred only one other person and finished second-last overall. I had felt the rush of competition and suddenly being passionate about a sport that favoured a limp wrist didn't seem so silly after all. I was hooked.

Mr. Nelson tried to negotiate a compromise with my dad, his boss, as I cried because I couldn't go to the tryouts for the Prince Edward Island-bound provincial foil team. "I hafta … *sniff* … go play a … *sniff* … basketball tournament —" I looked away, embarrassed to meet Mr. Nelson's eyes— "in Barnwell." As much as I may have wanted to ditch my basketball team for the chance to get a free trip to PEI, no daughter of Principal Oswald Schalm abandons her commitment to basketball in search of individual glory, especially in a sport like fencing, which did not have a rich tradition in Canada, let alone Brooks, Alberta. Finally my dad conceded that if I wanted to be on the provincial fencing team so badly, then I could attend the tryouts on the following weekend. The only problem: I'd miss the foil tryouts. But I could attend the tryouts for *épée*.

What's the difference, I hear you asking. Both are fencing sports ... if you are good at one, you should be good at the other. That's actually like saying a sprinter should be able to tackle marathons and vice versa because both are running sports. As with track, each fencing discipline is very different from the other in tactics, timing and attitude. Foil demands fast action, simply because the rules state that only the fencer with "priority" can score a hit. A fencer can take priority by attacking first, or by parrying an attack and then executing a riposte (a return attack, which is different than a counter-attack. Counter-attacks are when you respond to an attack by attacking right *into* their attack without parrying or otherwise defending). Attacks, parries, ripostes and counter-attacks can come so fast and furious that foil fencers tend to want to make their actions clear and obvious—it is the referee, after all, who decides the priority. You can make a hit, but that hit can still be annulled if the referee decides that you did not have priority.

Épée is quite different—more of a waiting game, since priority doesn't matter. A lead-up to a hit can seem to take forever, with each fencer waiting for the right time to attack. It's a discipline that requires a lot of interpretation of body language and can tend to attract people who are quite patient and cerebral. And in épée, the entire body, from head to toes, is a valid target. In foil, your target is the torso only. Many a foil fencer would argue that this means their discipline requires more accuracy and finesse—but perhaps they haven't tried to hit a knuckle on an opponent's weapon hand, or the toe of an agile foot.

In the end, of course, both foil and épée require stamina,

courage, and control. But the differences can seem enormous when a fencer tries to switch from one to the other. Changing swords was quite traumatic since it demanded a change in attitude and thinking. However, in the end it all worked out because, to be honest, I wasn't very good at foil. I loved analyzing people's body language and seeing what made them uncomfortable on the piste, which made me a more natural épée fencer. Women's foil had been around since the 1920s, but women have only been fencing épée competitively since 1989. This really put me in on the ground floor, and there was nowhere to go but up. Considering my athletic career up to this point (I was now 14), I was used to being an underdog and was excited about the challenge.

So I had one week to learn how to fence épée. As much out of desperation to succeed as the good graces of God, épée came quite naturally to me. The next weekend I qualified for Team Alberta and was headed to the Canada Winter Games! What an experience for a kid from Brooks. I couldn't shut up. "Is this your first time on an airplane? Me, too!" "Is this your first time doing an all-u-can-eat shrimp competition? Me, too!" "Is this the first time you've vomited in public? Me, too." "Is this your first time winning a gold medal?" It was a great learning experience and I made a lot of lifelong friends. By now these friends know the truth: until that point I had never won a gold medal, and it was not my first time vomiting in public.

Before I left for the big show, Mr. Nelson gave me one of his pep talks: "Sherraine, you can geh-a meh-al at this thing, really you can!" I nodded in agreement but all I was thinking was, "I wonder how many free cokes I can I drink during a four-hour flight?" A week later his words came back to haunt me. At the end of the individual competition I had finished fourth overall and I remembered Mr. N's jawing. I wondered to myself, "If I had really put some brains behind this, could I have come away with a medal?" This kicked me into gear for the team event, and after an exhausting joint effort, we won gold. It was a glorious moment and each team member had her own way of celebrating. Jennifer

Carroll called her parents. I toddled off to the cafeteria and ate an inordinate amount of Fudgsicles. Rebecca Williams, the strangest and most talented of us all, went and lopped off all her hair. We were shocked that she didn't seem to care what others thought, and even more shocked that she didn't seem to look in a mirror before she paid the hairdresser. After that I knew fencing was the sport for me. It offered travel, competition and good friends who were even weirder than I was.

The Long Arm of the Law

I f an individual sport was going to be my main focus, I would have to change some of my counterproductive habits. Until that point, team sports had been my priority because they seemed better suited to my sociability. In a team, talking incessantly is considered "communicating" which leads to "team building." Team sports also take away the emphasis on individual discipline; at the low levels, training is all run by your coach, and you either do it on the spot or you get kicked off the team! "Schalm, you're late—do 30 sprints ... Schalm, you missed that easy pass—do 30 push-ups ... Schalm, you've been eating too many nachos—give me 30 sit-ups." As a teenager, the horror of being rejected by my peers drove me to train without complaint; with fencing you have to push *yourself*.

School didn't develop my hard-working, disciplined attitude either; my parents had gifted me with enough grey matter that I could pull off decent grades without sweating. Come to think of it, it was the fine arts that brought to light my complete lack of focus and revealed the first stretch of the road to an athlete's work ethic. In school, I remember filing into the gym to hear a motivational speaker utter the words: "If you cheat yourself in the dark, it is going to show up under the lights." I never really knew what that meant, and I was pretty sure that I was too young to be doing any cheating in the dark anyway. The phrase finally made sense to me at age 15 as I sat slumped over a piano in the Medicine Hat College auditorium, my face burning with shame.

I had been taking piano lessons since age six with Mrs. Ramona Van Tol. Everybody has their own "my music teacher is weirder than yours" story to tell, so I won't try to outdo any of you here. She would have been fully appreciated anywhere but Brooks. How could she share her vast knowledge of music with a community who only wanted to hear Shania Twain's newest single or the new Oak Ridge Boys CD? I was lucky enough to be privy to her insights: "Robert Schumann died because he went crazy. All he could hear in his head was this note," she would say, her eyes widening to increase the drama as she struck A-flat at least twenty times. The thought of a composer being haunted to death by a *note* creeped me out and confirmed that I was nowhere near tortured enough to become a great artist.

Before I'd even had a lesson, my mother had booked a parent-teacher interview and went to see Mrs. Van Tol. "Don't worry about Jonene," she said (my sister was also starting piano lessons at the same time). "She will do what you say and is very well behaved. With Sherraine, however, you shouldn't hesitate to, um, lay down the law." Now Mrs. Van Tol may have heard what my mom said, but I don't believe she actually listened. Amid endless chit-chat and laughter we became fast and life-long friends. Over time our lessons stretched longer and longer. During my high school years we were up to hour-and-a-half-long lessons but she only charged for 45 minutes each. She couldn't justify making my parents pay for the time that she and I would spend chatting.

She had a gift for making people laugh, even at the most absurdly horrible situations. When I went away to university, Mrs. Van Tol would send me letters painstakingly written on her type-writer, keeping me up to date on the goings-on in Brooks. "My brother Fernando's dog was killed. He shot it thinking it was a coyote. His wife wanted him to get a new one as quick as possible but he told her, 'If *you* died, I wouldn't be running all over the county looking for a new wife. I need some time to grieve, woman!'" And then another time her letter began, "Dear Sherraine, I lost two students this year. Death got them."

She was the rarest of women, a wonderful role model who appreciated people's individuality. She didn't listen to the snide comments of others, only putting worth in the opinions of those people she respected. My weekly lessons with her were a treasured part of growing up. Her strict side came out in the comments she would write in my dictation book which without fail were along the lines of, "Sherraine MUST spend more time practicing!" This was a source of tension between me and my parents, especially when I was taking my Royal Conservatory exams. These were serious recitals judged by trained professionals who penalized you for even *thinking* about playing the wrong note. Until my ill-fated sixth year of Royal Conservatory, I coasted by thanks to my decent ear for music and modest talents. In year six the musical pieces were a lot longer and much more difficult, and for the first time had to be performed from memory. As she saw with increasing horror that I was still unable to play through any of my selected pieces, Mrs. Van Tol gave me a cassette with a recorded version played by professionals. She meant for me to use it as a supplement for my practice. I meant to use it as an escape from practice.

With my new wonder-cassette, my practice time could be shaved down to 10 minutes of scales. I would put my ghetto blaster (this was the '80s and so it was still called that) behind the piano, and after my scales were finished, I could sit back, push "play" and let the pros do my practicing. Of course I was no idiot to try to convince my parents, who just might actually be listening, that I could play *that* well, so I would stop the tape every now and then, play a few mistakes on the piano after some frustrated mumbling, and push "play" again, sitting back and relaxing with my newest *Sweet Valley High*.

"Sounds lovely, sweetie!" My mom, our family's very own Tony Robbins!

"Doesn't sound too bad, I guess," my dad said gruffly, walking up from tying fishing flies in the basement. Ah, perfectionist Dad.

We drove all the way to Medicine Hat so I could play my pieces for an examiner of the Royal Conservatory of Canada. All the excuses in the world could not wipe the look of incredulous disgust from his face as I shrugged my shoulders after failing to play through *any* of my pieces. Normally people take Royal Conservatory exams for one of two reasons: they are seriously pursuing a musical career or they are being pressured by over-achieving parents who need their child to be the best in everything. I fell into neither category, but when my music grades came in the mail several weeks later and my dad saw the abhorrent word "Fail," I could finally relate to the expression "parental pressure." I had to retake the exam, and this time "Oz" was deter-mined that I would pass. I did, no questions asked and no cassette tapes used.

Now don't get carried away thinking that suddenly because some pursed-lipped, wiry-haired piano examiner knocked me down a few pegs that I became a perfectly disciplined athlete with no flaws. There were still many moments in training when Mr. Nelson had to bribe me with Slurpees to get me to do a few more lunges. But failing my piano exam and then working hard to pass it later taught me a basic lesson important to any serious athlete: at the high levels, talent isn't nearly enough.

Getting Serious

When I was about 15 years old, Mr. Nelson saw that I was finally through the "giggle years," which usually precede the more dangerous "angst years." He thought it was a good time to develop me into a *serious* athlete. He sat me down one day and said, "Sherraine, yuh can take this sport all the way to the top if yuh want. National team, Olympics and maybe one day, even beat me." I was sure he was kidding. Beat him? This was probably just another ploy to get something, like how he conveniently organized our after-school practices to end just before dinner. "Oh, come on in, Alan! How are you? Why as a matter of fact, we're just about to have dinner. Would you like to join us? No, it's no trouble! We just appreciate your dropping Sherraine off at home!" My scepticism was mainly owing to the fact that, while my parents had always been encouraging and positive, I don't remember any of my other coaches or teachers ever telling me that I could be the best in anything, except maybe number of words said per minute. I had entered fencing with the innocent intentions of hanging around Mr. Nelson, not to actually become the best at it!

"But Jonene plays basketball." This was my only response to Mr. Nelson's suggestion that I really focus wholeheartedly on fencing.

"Listen kid, I'm telling yuh, yuh can be really, really good if yuh give it everything! Forget what yuh sist-uh does." Mr. Nelson was obviously an oldest child.

I was torn and decided to try to do both sports with equal effort. Things finally came to a head when I had double-booked a basketball and fencing tournament. My parents, who were still doubtful about this new-fangled sport of fencing, agreed that I couldn't miss basketball. They drove me directly from winning the fencing competition to the middle of a basketball game. I jumped out on the court eager to prove that I could be a fencer *and* keep up with Jonene on the court. After a few minutes of running around, the gym started spinning and I began to see black spots. My coach, Mr. Hartley, called a time out and I staggered over to the bench and sat down. "What's wrong, are you hyperventilating? Are you fainting?" he asked.

"Get … me … a … muffin." In the excitement of winning the fencing competition, I hadn't eaten anything all day. Once the scene was over and I had scarfed down an oatmeal muffin, I felt ready to take the court again. But there and then I made a choice of which sport I would pursue. Becoming the best requires commitment, and it was a tough decision. I weighed my fondness for both basketball and fencing, scored my ability and talent in both and then multiplied the scores by the number of different countries I could visit doing each sport. Fencing easily came out the winner. Sorry, Jonene!

At the end of every school day I would train. I practiced footwork, took lessons (which consisted of repeating moves with my coach as target) and then had a few bouts and I waited to become *the best*. I waited. And I waited. Mr. Nelson took me to competitions; sometimes I won but most times I didn't. I kept wondering how many competitions I had to win before I was considered the best. One day Mr. Nelson told me with pride that I was currently the "highest ranked unclassified fencer" in Canada. That was good, but it certainly didn't make me the best, because there were still classified fencers who were ranked higher than I was. The quest continued.

By the time I was 16, I was ranked well enough to make the Under 20 Junior National team. This was an accomplishment! However, the Junior World Championships are a self-funded event. My parents are certainly not stingy, but they are limited financially. While they could manage to foot the gas bill for trips to Saskatoon, they did not have the income to buy last-minute flights to Italy, even for a cause like the World Championships. So began the entrepreneurial aspect of becoming a serious fencer in Canada. I began making visits to local business people. I had always been pretty good at selling things, which probably came from the heaps of praise I received from Jonene when we were young. When I was nine, Mom gave me permission to tag along with Jonene as she went to the mall to sell chocolate-covered almonds for band class. Once she realized that she would have to approach total strangers for money, she began the first of her Sherraine Affirmation sessions: "You are so much better at it than I am, Sherraine! People think you're cuter!" When I hesitated, she would think fast: "I'll give you a free box for every five cases you sell …" She knew how to get me every time. But selling yourself to business people as a high-level athlete with a legitimate need for hundreds of dollars is tougher than convincing some Zeller's shopper to buy a two-dollar box of almonds, so at this early stage Mr. Nelson did most of the talking.

We rounded up enough money to get me to the World Junior Championships (to be held in Genoa, Italy, back in 1992). I could feel it: if I did well at this tournament, I would finally become the best! There was nothing in my way now, until the Canadian Fencing Federation told me I couldn't compete. They had neglected to mention that I had qualified only because the girl ranked ahead of me decided not to go. When she changed her mind and decided to go to the Worlds two weeks after I had already collected the money, I was stuck with a pre-paid plane ticket courtesy of IGA, Ropp's Pet Store, and Excalibur Drilling. I decided to go anyway to get a look at the fencing big leagues, and maybe see inside an Italian disco. It was a good decision because it not only gave me an idea of what went on at an international tournament, but for the first time I saw people from different countries who spoke different languages competing together under the same rules. There is something inexpressibly moving about seeing people your age from a totally different culture, all driven by the same passion you are. You feel part of a special order of athletes.

After being teased with the 1990 Junior World Championships, I finally made the team legitimately for the Under 17 Cadet World Championships which were held in Germany the following year. Finally, I could become the best! Well … let's just say that I certainly *tried* my very best, but to be honest, the girls there were just too good. I made it to the round of 32 (in direct elimination, the top 32 fencers), but then lost to a Brazilian girl. Watching the final matches, I realized that these were not 16-year-old girls who happened to do some fencing after school; they happened to go to school when they weren't fencing. One such testimony to the European's winning combination of talent and a fine sport system was Germany's Imke Duplitzer. She is a six-foot-tall Gatling gun who, at that time, probably trained more in one day than I did in a week. She dominated the piste. And if her size wasn't intimidating enough, she also had a bone-rattling victory yell. Even though she didn't win that particular World Championship, she is still the one to beat at most World Cup events nowadays.

Something started to dawn on me that day: I was only a big fish in a small pond. Even knowing that, I had to keep up my hope for success. I had to believe that I could still be the best or I wouldn't have the capacity to recognize it even when it happened. I felt crushed, but I hung on to that belief.

From this seed of faith came an understanding that has kept me sane. After winning a few times or even just having that over-

whelming desire to win, who was I? Was I defined by my achievements or was I someone whose worth ran deeper? Fencing has
given me many epiphanies because it's almost always in my
darkest moments that truth is illuminated. God is the only person
I have found who is unchanging, so that is where I place my
identity. Because of that stable place, I'm free to take risks and try
to be the best.

Around the World in a Daze

nternational travel was by far fencing's biggest perk. I didn't have to travel with the entire high school band, local travel club or my parents, but I did get to see the world with all my sports buddies. Go to Mexico, fight a few bouts, visit the pyramids with my friends, eat a fajita and come home. Go to Japan, fight a few bouts, sing some karaoke, have a tea ceremony with my friends, come home. There were worse things I could have done in my adolescence.

Travelling to compete as a 17-year-old in a developed country like Germany was a safe, if unrealistic, introduction to international travel. I had already been to Italy, but not to compete. The easiest place in the world to travel is Germany: it's not too expensive, it's safe, the trains run on time, bathrooms are clean and men don't pinch your bum. We travelled as a big group of athletes always under the coaches' watchful eye. In countries like Germany, if anything happened to go wrong, we knew that there was a responsible legal and policing system in place that would take care of innocent, harmless tourists such as ourselves.

This was not quite the case a year later when we travelled to Venezuela for the Pan American Junior Championships. The

Canadian contingent was smaller than usual and because of Canada's huge size and certainly not because of the heat of separatist tendencies, we travelled as two groups, the Westerners and the Easterners. We agreed to meet up in Merida, the host city located high in the Andes. Our flight plan had few stops: Calgary—Miami—Merida. As I have learned over time, travel is seldom without surprises.

It was a choppy flight over the ocean en route from Miami to Merida. After a few landing attempts in Caracas, the pilot decided that we would be safer landing in neighbouring Colombia. My eyes went wide. Safer? The only thing I knew about this country was a local legend that a high school teacher's sister had travelled there a few years ago and *she was never seen again.* My mind was all muddled with fear. Wasn't Colombia a country full of drug barons and mountain thugs who regularly kidnapped foreigners for impossible ransoms?

There was no connecting flight to Merida: because of the terrible weather, no flights were landing anywhere in Venezuela. We explained our urgency: one of our travelling companions had his competition the next day. So, the airline offered to hire a taxi to drive us to Merida. Moments after leaving the airport the five of us were squished into a taxi cab. The close quarters actually helped keep our spinal columns intact because our driver handled corners like one the Duke brothers.

Had Gandalf conjured up a car for Frodo to help him along his way, his trip through Middle Earth might have felt something like our drive from Colombia to Merida, Venezuela: lonely, desolate mountain stretches through guerrilla-ridden terrain. We had Gollum to lead us, too. Our taxi driver alternated between hating us because of our noisy Game Boy and sing-a-longs and being sickeningly sweet ("You are very nice people from Canada, no? You have the 'dinero' the airlines give you, no?"). He was excited to get rid of us but desperately wanting the bolivars we had been given to pay him when we reached our destination. The trip was broken up about every hour or so when the cab would scrape around a corner where the bamboo edged out onto the rutted dirt roads and we would meet a real life equivalent of the Black Riders. These men were either the mountain thugs I had dreaded or actual Colombian military police in charge of the road blocks, but either way, they were no English Bobbies. They dressed in camouflage uniforms and lovingly stroked their machine guns as they glared at us.

When we drove up to our first road block, my heart beat faster as I imagined arrest and detainment scenarios, hostage taking, or at least robbery. This is it, I thought. Now people in Brooks are going to tell campfire stories about when Sherraine the Fencer went down to Colombia, got in a taxi and, *was never seen again!* When the military police made us all get out of the car and stand with our backs against the doors, I thought, this is it. They are going to shoot us. This may sound like a panicky thought, but believe me, when you're in a foreign country and you experience a mosaic of safe, developed regions and less developed areas full of armed men, you can feel like you've stepped into a Hobbesian world where even the sight of police is frightening. When they made us pull out our passports and hold them open beside our faces I thought, *now* this is it. They are going to sell our passports, say that we have all gone missing, and we will *never be seen again!* Finally, they told us we could get back in the car. The stress of each roadblock shortened my lifespan by a few days as I imagined every bad thing that had ever happened in any scary movie I had ever seen. So my overactive teenage mind continued to panic for most of the eight-hour trip, calmed only when my friend Cameron would hand over his Game Boy.

When we finally made it to Merida, it was not a minute too soon, and we were equally surprised and annoyed to see the other group of Canadians who made it *sans problèmes.*

They probably arrived earlier than we did because they were more mature and much better travellers. They were also much cooler. They were bilingual, listened to techno music and under-stood fashion. I, on the other hand, was a social disaster. I only spoke English. I knew all the words to Roger Whittaker's greatest hits, including the duet he sang with Nana Mouskouri. And no one ever told me that safety pins at the bottom of my pants didn't look good. My late teens were, like most people's, all about struggling to fit in, or at least find a comfortable niche. This was still the case for me outside of school and in the fencing world. So, I put all my eggs in one basket and asked a guy named Cameron to hang out with me. Instead of getting to know my teammates and going through the cycle of initial politeness followed by impatience and finishing up with either mockery or the silent treatment, I spent my time with Cameron, who was definitely as weird as I was. This is the guy who didn't flinch when I accepted his dare and licked the park ranger's leg at a fencing camp in Jasper. And likewise, I didn't flinch when he started measuring distances with how many times he could sing Barry Manilow's "Copacabana." On one of the first days in Merida, Cameron and I ventured out into the downtown market area and came back with bags full of ceramics, bracelets and thick wool sweaters. We were feeling pretty accomplished now that we had seen the city on our own. No one could call us back-woods fools, even if we *were* from Alberta! One of the very sophisticated French Canadian girls who had never noticed us before now came rushing over excitedly, "Oh, were you already in de market?"

"Yes," we said, hesitating. I saw Cameron resist the urge to share with her that it was only six Copacabanas away. Was my social circle actually going to grow?

"Did you see any pot?" she asked inquisitively.

We nodded energetically, anxious to impress her. "Sure! We saw lots of different kinds of pots: ceramic, glazed, painted. Practically everyone was selling them! They're pretty hard to take across customs, but if they confiscate it at least you've only lost a few bolivars!"

"No, I mean *pot*, like de kind you smoke, not for cooking tings," she condescended.

"Oh, of course," we said, recovering. "We knew that, you know. Anyway, gotta go, these sacks are getting heavy, so many pots in them—ha ha! See ya at supper!" We scurried off around the corner before breaking out into laughter, partly at ourselves and partly at her.

As with most international travel, by the time the trip came to an end we were ready to get home where we could understand the locals and drink the tap water. Thankfully, on the return trip there was no eight-hour taxi ride. We exchanged that little inconvenience for three days shut up in our Miami hotel room watching reruns of the *Golden Girls*. The hurricane that had met us on the way down to South America had followed us back north and we were trapped in Miami. We amused ourselves by cracking open and eating the coconuts that had been blown off the palm trees and left by the hotel's pool ... which, by the way, was not even one Copacabana away from our room.

Even considering that Colombian trip, travelling was pretty easy as a junior. It was more intense as I became better at fencing and entered university in 1993 when I was 18. When I was getting ready to leave Brooks to go to university, Mr. Nelson talked to my parents and said that he knew of a great coach in Ottawa: someone who was a fencing master, a former Olympic coach, and above all, a very respectable man. By then I had already been accepted at the University of Alberta, chosen my courses and found an apartment. But father Oz came through again. If there was a better option for one of his children in pursuing sports, Oswald was not going to pass it up, and to be honest, neither was I.

Within two weeks I had been accepted at the University of Ottawa. We talked to the coach and I bought a one-way plane ticket to Ottawa where I started my real education. Outside of swordplay, I wasn't really clear on a career path, so I took courses in Shakespeare's works, molecular biology and European history, trying to get a taste of everything that interested me. My decision to do Teachers' College came much later (in 2000). The biggest sacrifice in changing schools was the time spent with friends and family—Dad received a whopping five-hundred-dollar phone bill after my first month on my own in Ottawa. After a few months of adjustment, getting my BA was a blast. I made a lot of great friends from the fencing club, my classes and church; I came to love a new city; and eventually met my husband there.

My studies naturally involved a lot of cross-training, under the tutelage of Paul ApSimon, the assistant coach at the time. Most of this took place in a pub after the fencing training. First of all I had to learn to play billiards to improve the extension of my fencing arm. Darts was pure hand-eye coordination training, and the early-morning greasy spoon breakfasts were fuel-ups for those long bouts. It would have been challenging with all those distractions to stay on the Junior National team and also qualify for the senior team. Luckily, my new coach was everything Mr. Nelson had promised.

Manuel Guittet was an ex-pat like Mr. Nelson, but he hailed from Paris, France. He fell in love with a Québécoise journalist in 1976 and has been in Canada ever since. He speaks English, French, German, Spanish and Chinese. He is a concert pianist. He is a doctor of mathematics. He is one of the few fencing masters who can give fencing lessons with both his left and right hand to two fencers ... *at the same time*. Under his tutelage, I became delightfully unaware of whether my opponent was left- or right-handed. This is a huge advantage in fencing where many of the top girls are left-handed. There have been theories claiming that, unlike right-handers, lefties have cross-dominant vision, which gives them a keener depth perception and helps their ability in sports like fencing and tennis. There is also a theory that it is simply a numbers advantage—only in this case an advantage for the minority. It's rare to find a left-handed fencer in your average club or competition, and as a result most fencers get used to training with and competing against right-handed opponents. When suddenly faced with a lefty, who has reversed techniques and different distance, they may not know how to handle them. So while only about 10 percent of the general population is left-handed, forty percent of the top 10 women's épéeists in the world are left-handed. It is a big advantage to be at ease with both right- and left-handed fencers.

Looking back on those years, I really loved training with Manu, especially when it was at his house. He and his wife have a beautiful home in a chic part of Ottawa, which gave me a much-needed reprieve from the student ghetto where I lived during university. On rainy or cold days we would have lessons in the piste he had created in his basement. In the summer, he gave me lessons beside his backyard pool.

Before I would leave for World Cups in other countries, Manu would have me make two goals: one competitive, the other cultural. I would aim to finish in a certain round at the competition, and also find one interesting cultural experience in that country. Thanks to this balanced approach, I have been caving in Budapest, toured the Palace of Versailles near Paris, spent an afternoon in the Munich *biergartens* and choked down blood sausage in Argentina. Hey, I never said they were all pleasant, just cultural. During one of many trips to Europe, Manu and I visited some kind of museum of technology in Heidelberg. He was always very interested in old instruments, and when we came into the piano section of the museum he almost passed out from hyperventilation he was so excited. There was a woman there tuning the pianos and tinkering around a bit when Manu shyly sidled up to her. "Do you think I could play a little bit?" he asked in German.

"Well, normally we don't let anyone play these. Except me, of course, I am the extremely important piano tuner. I have to keep these pieces in fine working order for nobody to play. As for you playing, this is a museum, not a factory, sonny. And this is Germany, not Never-Never Land. But ... since you look sheepish and shy and I feel I can dominate you, I guess if you played just a little, I wouldn't be too angry," she said. I don't speak German, but her intonation and body language were easy to translate.

Manu assessed the sheet music that she had lying around,

hoping for a challenging piece. I still wonder if the pieces were real museum props, facsimiles of composer's notes or just papers the woman brought with her everyday to impress the people walking by. "Wow, can she really play that?" the museum-goers would ask each other as they stared at Chopin's notation, which was so complicated and crazy that it looked like a Jackson Pollock painting. When Manu asked me to turn the pages for him I knew it would be next to impossible to actually read the music, so I became Clever Hans the counting horse. Instead of doing real math, I just watched, unblinking, as Manu played. When he gave a terse nod I flipped the page.

If Manu had been less concerned with beauty and more concerned with economy, he could have charged admission. While he was playing, museum goers kept coming into the room to watch and listen, mouths agape at how suddenly an artifact came to life, living its purpose of transmitting beautiful music to the soul. I finally understood why Manu was always pushing the cultural aspect of travel. The whole world was full of glimpses of eternal beauty, and if you weren't aware of them, they would slip by unappreciated.

Because Manu was a doctor of seemingly everything, I thought that there was no way I could ever teach him anything. What travel with me *did* teach him, however, was how to perfect his ability to talk his way out of trouble. This was my gift to him.

Before leaving on my first trip to Cuba I had heard horror stories of "tourist" disease, shark bites and petty theft. I was 19, and once there, I took what I thought to be all the necessary precautions. I had been warned that the water was unfit to drink so I went so far as to shower with my eyes closed. I had learned that the waves were very dangerous, so I only waded knee-high. And I had learned that many people were trying to flee the country so to be sure, I hid my passport in the safest place I knew: under my mattress.

"Manu, I don't have my passport."

"What? Where is it? Did it get stolen?"

Sherraine MacKay

"I, uh, left it behind."

"Where? In the bus?"

"No, at the hotel."

"If it is in the hotel safe, they could probably deliver it," he calculated quickly, "but we would be tight for time ... our flight leaves in an hour!"

"Actually ..." I hesitated, not wanting to tell him where I had left my passport. "It's somewhere in my room, but I don't really know where ... exactly ..." I said vaguely.

As recovering my passport seemed hopeless to them now, Manu and the team manager Jacques Cardyn went straight to work on the Cuban customs officials. If I missed this charter flight I would have to catch the next one, which was in one week! In fluent Spanish, they wheeled and dealed with the customs people while I looked as innocent and dimwitted as possible, which, given the situation, wasn't such a stretch. I showed the identification I had on me, my non-photo Alberta health card and a Blockbuster membership card. In the end, they decided to let me out of the country, either because they could tell that I was not a Cuban on the run or because even if I was Cuban, I was too stupid to keep in the country's gene pool. From there our main concern was with the Canadian customs office, which would never let someone into the country without papers no matter how authentically they said "about." As it turned out, for the first and only time in my life there were absolutely no customs officers on duty; it was 4:00 a.m. The only person between our border and the rest of the world was a flight attendant sullenly collecting customs forms as people filed by to get their luggage. I breathed a sigh of relief, but I must admit I had a twinge of concern for our national security.

I had a bigger scare a few months later when, new passport in hand, I was watching the Pan American Games fencing final held in Argentina. The Cuban team was sitting right in front of us and I noticed something had fallen on the floor. It was a Canadian passport. I looked at my coach and gawked, "Now who would be careless enough to drop their passport on the gym floor? Don't people realize how important a passport is?" I opened it and found I was staring at my own face. Somehow my *old* passport had found its way from between the mattress springs of room 202 at Hotel Tropicoco in Cuba to the gym floor in Mar del Plata, Argentina. How the … what the … ? A million thoughts rushed to mind. Did one of the Cubans find this and plan to sell it? Was one of them travelling illegally on my old passport and hoping to defect? Did I really once weigh that much? I rushed over to our manager, Jacques Cardyn, and explained the situation. He was very concerned and told me to go confront the Cuban team immediately. "Go get them! Obviously one of them stole it, and now they're travelling around as you. You've got to stop them Sherraine! Take back your identity! Do it!" he said with a clenched fist smacking his palm.

Now feeling just as threatened as I did inspired, I walked off slowly toward where Team Cuba was watching the final. All of a sudden I found an excuse for not doing this alone—I couldn't speak Spanish! As I turned to ask for Jacques' or Manu's help, I found them laughing hysterically and high-fiving.

"What," I asked, "are you doing?"

"There are no Cubans with your passport, Sherraine," Jacques said. "I placed it there. The hotel in Cuba sent me your passport a while ago, so Manu and I thought we would teach you a lesson. By the way Sherraine, mattresses are only good hiding places in prisons and summer camps!" That was how Manu repaid me for the one lesson I was able to teach him.

Going through customs gives you telltale signs of the general behaviour found in each country. Border guards often give some indication of what certain countries are like. Many years ago when I was trying to collect as many stamps as possible in my passport, I was going into Switzerland for a World Cup. The customs officer gave a quick but thorough look at my documents and handed it back to me without marking it. I slid it back toward him. "Excuse me, do you think you could give me a stamp?" I asked in my cutest voice. The Swiss official didn't speak "cute." He flipped his head up to see who dared to ask him a question and in a superior tone said, "What do you think this is, a post office?" before taking my passport and very carefully and neatly stamping it.

On that same trip I drove through Liechtenstein, the world's smallest country (don't tell me you actually consider Vatican City a country). The border guard was very nice and didn't even seem insulted when he asked how long we were going to be in the country and we said, "Just the 25 minutes it takes to drive through it, sir!" I thought it would be pretty original to have a passport stamp that is almost as big as the country itself, so before we drove away I asked if he could give me one. The guard walked back to the office but returned empty-handed, shrugging his shoulders. "I'd love to lady, but we don't even have a stamp!" I wondered whether casualness was an official country policy, and later, it was confirmed that this refreshing attitude came straight from the top. In the Liechtenstein tourist bureau, I picked up the official royal family postcard which showed the whole royal family, posed beautifully on a decorative staircase ... all spiffy in jeans and denim shirts. If I hadn't looked at the flipside that said "Royal Family of Liechtenstein" they could have been confused for the cast of *Family Ties*.

Smoking is a Food Group?

During my university years, women's épée was inducted into the Olympic Games, in Atlanta, 1996. This opened up a whole new world for me because until then, the Olympics had just been a quadrennial excuse to get out of weeding the garden for two weeks in the summer. Now the Olympics had become the ultimate international stage for my sport. Over the past few years, I had qualified for several large-scale multi-sport games (the World University Games, Pan American Games, et cetera) and I had developed a taste for the hype that went along with them. I loved eating breakfast in the Athletes' Village with the Canadian rowers, wrestlers and basketball players knowing that we were going out there that day to give it our all, hoping to become the very best. It was motivating to be grouped with highly trained athletes who had the same lofty goals. At these big events, the girls I had fenced with all year long on the World Cup circuit were suddenly a little more nervous, extremely intense and hungry for victory as they tested themselves on a higher level than ever before. I wanted to experience that intensity at the greatest athletic show on earth: the Olympics.

Sherraine MacKay

However, my level of training was still not where it needed to be for me to consider myself a high-performance athlete. I had no concept of what I should eat, how much rest I needed or how much physical preparation I had to do. When the Canadian team did not win the zonal qualifier, we lost our chance to compete in the team event at the Olympics. Teams that are not ranked in the top four in the world must qualify in one of four "zones" in order to gain a berth at the Olympics. At that time, teams had to either finish in the top eight at the World Championships the year before the Olympics or, win the competition held in each zone—Europe, Asia-Oceania, America, and Africa—a few months prior to the Olympics. Failing that, an individual fencer could gain an Olympic berth by being ranked among the top two individuals in her zone, but that didn't help me much either. Qualifying in a zone means gaining one of the two highest world rankings in that zone, and I was nowhere near that level individually. I wouldn't be going to the Olympics in Atlanta—I just wasn't good enough yet. It was back to the drawing board and looking toward Sydney 2000.

As I looked at my options, I felt like Joan of Arc being told by God in a dream to lead her country into battle. Actually, it was Manu telling me over pizza one night that if I wanted to get to the next level I should go train in France. By about this time in my life my siblings had all started families, and I became the pilgrim auntie coming into town every few years, bringing gifts from strange countries and demanding a hug even though my nieces and nephews were more familiar with the local Safeway clerk than with me. Fortunately, my family has been understanding and quite creative in their attempts to keep my image alive and well in their children. My existence was sustained through photos and stories: "When your Auntie Shep (yes, they call me Shep) was your age, she ran around the garden with her underwear on her head! Here's a picture of it!"

Manu explained that in France the coaching was good, I could get better sparring and that he could set me up in a training centre. He said I would see what it takes to get to the top. But he never mentioned anything about loneliness, eating disorders and depression.

He arranged for me to work with one of his friends: Jean Michel, a former Canadian national coach and a fellow fencing master who was coaching at the National Training Centre in Bordeaux. So in October 1998, when I went to the World Championships in Switzerland, I caught a train to Bordeaux instead of the airplane home with the rest of the Canadian team. Once I arrived, I began to see why fencing was consistently France's highest medal hope at the Olympics: they train non-stop! When I first arrived at the training centre, the medical team took one look at me and ushered me into their test room. They put a plastic mask on my face, placed suction cups all over my body and made me run on a treadmill until I dropped. Once I was on the floor, they told me to do as many sit-ups as I could manage. When I rolled over onto my stomach, vomiting up whatever I had eaten in the last day, they said, "Pair-fect, now you are in ze good position to do push-ups, so try to keep ze same rhy-zem as ze beeps." I think I may have heard two beeps before I felt ready to pass out. So this was high-level training in France … I think I know how those kids feel on Jerry Springer who get sent to boot camp for delinquency. Only this was not boot camp and Jerry Springer was nowhere in sight; it was just the pre-training physical test. The real Jerry Springer episode started when they measured my body fat. Five men selected the gooiest parts of my body, where they nipped and pressed, measuring my fat with steel calipers. They alternated between pinching and madly writing down numbers until they were satisfied. I wasn't what you would consider obese, but for a high-level athlete I was clearly sub-par. This assessment also reflected the French culture; clothing sizes don't go beyond 10, and most of the population considers smoking a major food group. I was told to trim down.

Smoking aside, the French are relatively healthy and they defi-nitely know how to eat. France is not a country of crash diets and fasting. Lunch brought in a paper bag is sacrilegious and in some schools I've heard they will make you eat the bag. Children, athletes, businesspeople, even the homeless can regularly sit down to a hot lunch. Since they have been raised to eat three healthy meals per day with no snacks in between (barring the odd Marlboro and short, strong coffee, of course) they don't seem to have weight problems. If they are trying to lose a little weight, they wouldn't even consider eating grapefruits and celery from dawn until dusk. This country produces more than three hundred types of cheese and even more varieties of wine; they could never limit themselves to food that has not been given the proper time to ferment. If they are on a diet, they just eat *less* steak, green beans and baguette than usual and exercise a little more. In Paris, exercise could be anything from jogging through the Tuileries garden in leather loafers to walking home from the opera. At the training centre in Bordeaux we were sent on runs through the forest on the assumption that we would get lost and would have to follow up with a long, desperate walk back. We all ate together at the communal cafeteria, where I was under the watchful eye of my training partners. "She took extra bread," they would whisper in French, looking at me and smiling sweetly if I caught their eye. "She took cheese *and* yoghurt!" Snicker, snicker, while I was sitting there oblivious to what they were saying because I hadn't yet learned the language. In spite of having no real intention to do so, the peer pressure and the stress of my new, painful situation made me lose enough weight to make me lighter on the piste and more acceptable in the eyes of my training partners.

My weight loss was done by the book, in terms of reduced calorie intake and healthy meal choices, because at a training centre it is hard to go wrong. It's not like the chefs were preparing Duck a l'Orange every night. It was more like cold turkey slices and white rice. The orange, you peeled for dessert. The pounds came off, but for all the wrong reasons. Sadly enough, the desire to attain healthier weight and get in better condition for fencing was not my only motivation. I was also making a last-ditch effort to fit in. I did not yet speak the language and I had very few friends. So, contrary to everything I had grown up believing, I started to think that if I was just a little thinner and more beautiful, the other girls and guys would like me more. Usually females go through this crisis in their teen years but my family, coach and friends had been such a solid support group I had never worried about my physical appearance. I just knew that they would like me for who I was. Don't misunderstand me, I do believe that a high-level athlete has to be in the best possible shape with a minimum amount of body fat, but like anything else in training, it must come from a healthy motivation that does not in any way suggest that the more you weigh, the less of a person you become.

Here in France, it seemed different. There was much more pressure on women to be as thin as possible, and whether it was real or imagined, I felt alienated and too ugly to have friends. I had gone to school with the same friends from kindergarten to Grade 12, so I never wondered who I was going to sit with on the bus or who would share my swimming locker with me. In Bordeaux, I clearly remember having my first moment of social panic as I walked from the line to the cafeteria tables. There I was a 20-year-old, working hard at becoming the best in the world, and all that was going through my head was, "Please let there be someone who wants to sit with me!"

Weight is a sensitive issue for most people, and it hits female athletes especially hard. There are non-stop comparisons between women from the moment you walk in the gym to when you sit down for a meal. In France, especially at a training centre, there are so few overweight people. The thinner you are, the more you are admired for your discipline and good looks. This pressure drove me crazy because, even though I had lost about 10 pounds, my male friends would look at me and shake their heads wondering aloud how I could be an athlete and be so fat.

In 1999 I came to train in Paris, and I was living alone without too many friends in a small studio space that my coach, Jean Michel, was kindly renting to me at half his usual price for the months I was training there. The coach and vice-president of the club announced loudly that I still needed to lose five pounds ... on each side of my butt. Sure, I needed to be lighter on the piste for an ease of movement and increased speed, and I completely agree that it is the coach's responsibility and right to be concerned about whether his or her athlete's physique is counterproductive to performance. However, there is a humane way of telling a woman that she would perform better if she lost a few pounds, and it does not include public announcements and the word "fatty."

I may have lost weight out of fear, but the French style of negative feedback had an extremely adverse affect on my emotional health. I would diet like crazy, consuming way too few calories, and then when I had a few moments alone, I would binge on whatever chocolate I could get my hands on, eating until I couldn't even taste it. Even though I didn't have a full-blown eating disorder, my friends and family would say that I had an eating obsession because I talked constantly about weight, food and how hard it was to maintain good habits. I had to work off any indulgence with more exercise as I constantly obsessed over my figure. My weight and figure had become my sad, new-found way to become the best.

Honestly, this has been a huge, ongoing battle that has only let up in the past year or so, as I have matured and learned to really listen to my body. There are some times when I need to eat more, and times when my body is telling me that I don't need as much fuel. After many sessions with a well-respected dietician / endocrinologist at the National Training Centre in Paris, I have finally established a balanced and healthy eating plan. Of course it is typically French: three solid meals per day, no bag lunches if I can help it. My snack food is fruit and I drink *lots* of water. (They didn't tap the mountains of Evian for nothing!) I've stuck with this plan because it allows for the pleasure of eating (this is France, after all), but with moderation (this is France, after all). I've quieted my obsession, attained and maintained my optimal weight, and I am finally in true high-performance athletic condition.

Sydney 2000

During the turbulent years of 1998 and 1999, I spent a total of about 10 months in Bordeaux and then Paris. I had finished my Honours BA in English in the spring of 1998 when I was 23. I moved to Bordeaux in October of 1998 and then Paris in late February 1999. In spite of all the culture shock and mental affliction, I improved quite a bit and ended up becoming the highest ranked person in the American zone (North and South America and everything in between), which was exactly what I needed to qualify individually for the Sydney Olympics. I came back to Ottawa for the last half of 1999 to catch my breath, relax, eat some poutine (pleasure of eating, remember?) and get ready for the World Championships in October in Seoul, South Korea. If I earned a good result there, I could practically guarantee my qualification for the 2000 Olympics.

Perhaps it was the positive atmosphere still in Seoul from when they hosted the 1988 Olympics, or perhaps it was the kimchi spicy aftertaste, but I felt like I was on fire going into the World Championships. I ended up having the best ever female World Championship result in Canadian fencing history, finishing sixth! I lost a heartbreaker in sudden-death overtime against the silver medallist, Switzerland's Diana Romagnoli. She is over six feet tall and her feet are bigger than my femurs, so tied at 14–14, I was sure I could smack 'em and win the match. I guess she is used to people trying for that target, because she saw me coming and easily hit my hand on the way in, winning and advancing to the medal round. Getting that close to the medals left me hungry for more victories, and they were coming.

Even though I had quite a few good results and had even won a World Cup leading up to my participation in the Sydney Olympics, there are no formulas for winning at the big show. There are so many variables at an event as huge as the Olympics, and to be able to successfully separate yourself from the situation you either have to be a master of your own ego or a complete simpleton. For better or for worse, I was neither. I ended up having a bye in the first round and losing my match in the second round. I finished 19th, which was a record by default because I was the only Canadian woman ever to compete at the Olympics in épée. I could have finished dead last and it still would have been a new national record.

Now, in my older, wiser years, I see that I was under-trained for Sydney. I pretty much ate whatever I wanted with no nutritional consideration and my lack of focus on my footwork meant I was nowhere near as quick and agile as I could be. However, I had a very good technical coach at the time (Manuel Guittet) and so my technique was on par with most other women épéeists in the world. My fencing style was all about counter-offence. If the person would not attack, I was in trouble. My game was actually pretty limited. There were a number of other fencers who were definitely stronger overall than I was. I had won a World Cup already, so it was not that I couldn't win on any given day, it was just that I was not yet consistently strong in all aspects of épée fencing.

In spite of an early loss, Sydney was a wonderful experience. I learned how to deal with the media which, for a low-profile sport like fencing, only becomes an issue in the few months leading up to the Games. Although infrequent, media attention can have a crushing impact at an event as big as the Olympics and in Sydney it really affected my preparation. With all the demands the media was making for my time and the nutty questions I was asked, I found a whole new respect for those superstars who deal with this every day. I can't imagine how many times someone like, say, Tiger Woods has had to answer the questions: How did you get started in your sport? What is your favourite sports moment? And have you ever poked anyone's eye out?

Sydney also taught me to enjoy the ride. Sometimes when you are a part of an event as huge as the Olympic Games, you get stressed out by that whole "the world is watching" mindset, so you forget to look around and absorb the great moments you are experiencing. I remember Brian Williams hosting countless Opening Ceremonies on CBC and saying, "Well, as I look down on the sea of Canadian faces I am trying to recognize some of our most renowned athletes and let me just try to find ... no ... can't find them. I guess they elected to stay back at the Village." I always wondered, "Who *are* these people that choose to stay in the Village while 10,000 of their colleagues are having a huge party? What do those athletes do instead of taking their front row seat at a free, two-hour concert? What was so magnetic about that Village?" Well, in Sydney I found out, as I, too, elected to stay at the Village. Put simply, if you attend the opening ceremonies, you can spend a good six to eight hours on your feet. That can tire you out for the next few days and I wanted to save every precious ounce of energy for my only day of competition, which was quickly approaching. I had a match to lose, you know!

In Sydney, the Canadian men's field hockey team was also resting up, but that certainly did not mean shutting up. "Hey, all you athletes staying behind, show your support and put on the official parade uniform and meet us in the Team Canada lounge to watch the live CBC feed of the ceremonies! We'll have our own celebration!" They were walking around our block of buildings giving orders to party. We all did as told, and when the Canadians marched in for the ceremonies we cheered our friends and team-mates on TV. Then one of the especially energetic field hockey guys made a suggestion that still makes me smile when I think about it. "We should have our own parade!" he beamed. "Everyone has their stuff on, I can get a flag … let's do it!" So all 30 of us went outside and chose Curtis Myden to be our flag bearer, a position he mutely accepted. We taped the flag to a field hockey stick and marched behind Curtis, our fearless leader. As he led us around the Canadian buildings, one of the more emotional field hockey players started singing "O Canada" in a throaty, tenor warble. We let him sing alone just long enough to let him think that we weren't going to join in. He started looking around in a panic until we bellowed out, "IN ALL THY SONS COMMAND!"

The few Canadian athletes who had remained in their rooms came out to wave their support and take pictures of this oddity. We marched on to the cafeteria where some Australians who were up for a laugh were standing respectfully at attention and applauding us as we passed by them, singing like a bunch of tipsy Irish tenors. We always hear about that cheesy patriotism in the media and in interviews with Olympians, but I'm telling you, it gets heartfelt and intense really fast. Now I know at least one thing Brian Williams doesn't; I know the real reason why athletes stay in the Village.

The last thing I learned at the Sydney Olympics was my hardest and most public lesson. I learned to appreciate the great-ness of every athlete at the Games. Sometimes Olympic sports look too weird, too easy or just too confusing on TV. Some people would put fencing in all three categories. Their usual reasoning is, "If I was a fencer, I would just wind up and smack my opponent's sword as hard as I could until he dropped it, and then I'd just wail on him!" I guess these people miss the point of the sport, which is to touch an opponent with the tip of the épée, not to increase their health insurance premiums. (Of course these are usually the same type of people who were an Atom hockey coach's nightmare.) I take for granted that I am among the very best in the world, and it would take someone *years* of training to reach this level. You can trust me when I say that every athlete at the Games is an expert at his or her sport. I know this thanks to my underwhelming Olympic experience fencing foil.

At the Sydney Olympics, the only way you could enter a team was if you had three people qualified. To allow for more teams without increasing the overall number of athletes, the International Fencing Federation, in its great wisdom, allowed teams to be made up of two athletes from one weapon and a third athlete of the same gender from another weapon. This created mix-and-match teams in which one member with little experience with a foil or an épée would be matched against an expert. I was one such member. There were two foil fencers who had qualified from Canada: Jujie Luan and Julie Mahoney. They needed a third female Canadian fencer to complete their team. I was the only other Canadian woman who had qualified, so if I could somehow completely change my tactics, timing and style in a few days and learn how to fence foil, we could all compete together in the team foil event. It was after my individual flop, so I figured, why not? What harm could it do? It's probably like riding a bicycle … you never forget. Actually, it was more like riding a bicycle backward down the highway, blindfolded, against traffic. Ready or not, after two days of foil practice I walked out into the stadium to the cheers of spectators who had naively come to see team foil at its Olympic best.

When I fence épée, I use what we call a "French" grip. The French, with their continental flair, call it a "straight" grip. The French grip is almost extinct in foil because the weapon has evolved into a real speed event where you hit and get hit on the back. Even with my B in high school physics I could figure out that if I was facing my opponent and they were still able to hit me on my back with a straight steel sword, they had some serious hand strength that was not possible with a French grip. To help achieve this remarkable strength and agility, a foil fencer will tend to use a "pistol" or "orthopedic" grip. Unlike the French grip, this grip is designed to be clutched, with the palm curled around an almost vertical grip, and the thumb on top. As a result, your hand is neatly tucked behind the guard, and the strength of your wrist and lower arm can be added to that of your hand. At the same time, you can flex your wrist freely without losing control of the tip of your blade. This is ideal in the application of a "flick," which is basically a whipping motion that bends the blade so much that the tip can make a clear impact on just about any surface—your opponent's back included.

But since French grip was all I knew, I had purchased foils with a French grip, which completely removed the option of the "flick." In épée, you are considered moronic if you don't hold your French grip at the very end. This method not only increases your reach by several inches, but gives you flexibility. In contrast, to hold your French grip with your hand snuggled up against the guard leaves you with most of the grip held along your wrist— which makes it abit hard for your wrist to bend, almost as if it has been splinted. Even worse, to hold a French grip at the end is completely forbidden in foil.

You can imagine my confusion as I stepped out onto the piste under the bright lights and loud cheers from the Olympic fans, adjusting my unfamiliar electric jacket and holding my foil at the butt end. My team mate Julie walked up, placed herself between me and the judge and discreetly told me that the judge could give me a warning and then take away a point if I continued to hold my grip as I was so accustomed. This being the first time I had heard this rule, I panicked and looked up guiltily at the judge. He was quite young looking and strangely familiar. Then it clicked and I realized that there was no way he was going to punish me for such a technicality. He was a former boyfriend of an old teammate from my junior years. I'd seen him as a pimple-faced teenager chasing desperately after my friend; today he turned a blind eye, just as I'd hoped.

We started the match: "*Prêt?*" the judge asked in French, which is the official international language for fencing. "Ready?"

I won't be ready for another 10 years, I thought, as my mind raced, trying to remember all the techniques I had learned in my two days of training. "*Allez!*" he yelled. And we were off. Within three minutes, Canada's most decorated female fencer became the official pin cushion of the Canadian team. Here I was, the ninth best women's épée fencer in the world, and I could only score 2 out of 17 hits in foil. This gave me a whole new respect for the hours of practice it takes to even make a respectable showing at the Olympics.

Like so many other things in life, you have to be able to take the good with the bad and there were clearly two sides to both winning and losing. Having won so many important matches in the past few years gave me a passion for performance, but the dark aspect of this experience was that unknowingly I began to ground my sense of self and pride in my victories. I am sure this happens to most athletes when they break through to the elite levels. For me, winning wasn't everything, it was the only thing.

I hate clichés. That's why, though I love to watch hockey, I can't stand the post-game interviews. You know them all by heart. The camera is unsteady as the player finally ducks down into the shot and a TSN announcer says, "So, you were outshot 60 to 12 and you managed to tip a weak point shot into your team's goal. How do you feel going into tomorrow night's playoff game?" The player tosses his sweaty hair, wipes his patchy beard with his sleeve and says something like, "Yeah, we just gotta keep pluggin' away and stayin' positive … We'll just go out there and give it 110 percent …"

The worst clichés are usually found on coffee mugs and fridge magnets. They're the ones that are meant to push you either to greatness or directly into a therapist's office. "Losing is not an option." "Second place is first loser." And my personal favourite: "Victory or Death." Along with wicker furniture and the way the French say "brownies," victory clichés are among my biggest pet peeves. This might surprise you, coming from an Olympian. Don't misunderstand me: I love winning, I dislike losing. But *needing* to win is a huge and debilitating trap for me, for anyone. All I *need* is to maintain balance in my life. That last cliché just slays me because unless you find yourself in the Australian outback wrestling with a venomous snake, Victory or Death is just so untrue! Do we really need to be reminded so aggressively to be the best? I believe that people are inherently dissatisfied with second place, otherwise kids wouldn't fight for their parents' attention and Mr. Forbes wouldn't have to make lists of any kind.

People have an obsession with winning and I hope there are enough therapists to go around for all the inevitable disappointments that it creates. This is nothing new; the need to win has had a long and glorious tradition especially in sport. In the ancient Olympic Games, there was no second prize. The winner received a lifetime exemption from taxes, as well as free admission to the box seats in Greek theatre and a beautiful laurel wreath to dry and use as a centrepiece. The loser was just left to dwell on his mistakes forever.

I understand disappointment for what it is: a proof of our greatness. Blaise Pascal said that "all the miseries of man prove his grandeur; they are the miseries of a dignified personage, the miseries of a dethroned monarch." When something is within our reach and we fail to achieve it, we all experience an overwhelming sadness because we know how great we could have been and how we were created for greatness. On the other side of things, achieving our goals gives an almost irresistible excitement and satisfaction. This feeling is so breathtaking that it's addictive, and experiencing it can soon become the goal in itself. The difference between striving to win and *needing* to win is like the difference between loving the great things about your child or loving your child only when they do great things. My journey in sport has taught me a lifetime's worth of lessons about striving to be the best without obsession and being able to see past the setbacks ... and I've never needed a victory aphorism stuck to the fridge door.

I'll Call You Popeye

Most athletes go through a slight depression after the Olympics. I've heard that if you win, it can be even worse, so I figure I will save that for my last year of competition. Trainers and sports psychologists put the blame on lack of goal setting. The media puts the blame on certain athletes "coming down" from supplements, and coaches blame the athlete for over-thinking. Almost every athlete I know, including myself, has a few weeks of post-Olympic melancholy that is unexplainable. It's a lot like the post-Christmas blues. You build up the event so much in your mind, but it all happens too quickly. In the Village, as with Mom's kitchen, there is non-stop food and everyone eats too much. And although we all make an effort to be one big, happy family, there are the undercurrents of tension that sooner or later turn into full-on arguments, and people drag up things that happened way too long ago. "You let my fish starve to death when I was at band camp and I am still in therapy to overcome my fear of abandonment!" And its Olympic equivalent: "You shouldn't have taken that foul in the last quarter of the zonal qualifier for Atlanta or we would have been at those Games and had some experience so we wouldn't be losing today!" To recover from this condition after the

Olympics, athletes, like those trying to cure the post-Christmas blues, usually start a new hobby or take a vacation.

My boyfriend at the time of the Sydney Olympics had been keeping tabs on my results and he knew I would need something to pick me up when I came back to Ottawa. He never does things halfway, so while the boyfriends of other Olympians had signed their depressed girlfriends up for cross-stitch classes or bought gift certificates for pedicures, Geordie bought me a diamond ring and asked me to marry him. My new hobby was going to be planning a wedding and my vacation would be our honeymoon. He is one smart man.

He wasn't always this smart. The first time we met, he thought my last name was "Epee" because my e-mail address was epee@hotmail.com. "Wow, I really liked that Sherraine Epee," Geordie said to his friend later that same night. His buddy laughed, "Her last name is Schalm, not Epee, you boob! *Épée* is the name of the sword!" Geordie didn't mind the mocking; he believed that one day my last name would be easy for him to remember because it would be the same as his. And he was right.

The first time I saw Geordie was at a church-sponsored event where he was leading the music. I had grown up in a church where the youth group was made up of me, my sister and Mark Jacobsen, whom I tortured as if he were my sister. I forced him to play house with me all afternoon in exchange for playing with his stupid Hot Wheels for a few minutes after church. So pickings were slim in the "Godly boyfriend" department. I was not used to seeing someone passionate for God who was outside of my own gene pool. Geordie's good looks made it hard to focus on his spiritual qualities; during most of the service, I tried to use my mental training techniques to keep my mind focused on God, who was, after all, the point of the singing. "Focus on God ... man, that song leader is good looking ... Focus on God ... wow, he is so good looking ... focus on, oh, thank God he is so good looking!" I gave up trying to concentrate on the spiritual and made a note to work on the mental aspect of my game before the Sydney Olympics.

Running With Swords

We met a week later at a spiritual retreat where he was once again leading the music, and I liked him immediately. So much so, in fact, that I played hard to get. Geordie played along willingly until I took it in the wrong direction—"My life is very fast paced, and it takes me all around the world as I pursue excellence, so there is little to no room for a boyfriend." He didn't want to play that game. There was genuine concern as I mentioned my well-laid plans to move to Paris for several years after I finished teachers' college. "Paris, Ontario?" he asked hopefully.

I scoffed, "No! Paris, France. It's the only place that's suitable for me to really pursue fencing. I want to be the best at it, I have a lot of goals, you know ..." My voice trailed off as I slipped into a fencing reverie, imagining those matches yet to be won and World Cup rankings yet to be reached. Considering that my first time living in France was an expensive, friendless turmoil, I never thought that I would be anxious to get back, but it seemed that Paris was the only reasonable option for me to really establish myself among the best in the world.

A shadow crossed Geordie's face as he digested this. He saw how intense I was. Was there a place for him in such a lifestyle? As we finished up our conversation, I can only guess what he must have been thinking. "This is over before it started! How am I going to date someone in Paris, France? I wouldn't have a car to pick her up with; I hate French movies; I would have to call the waiter *garçon*, and he sure as heck wouldn't serve us spicy chicken wings. This'll never work." We had a nice weekend chatting and playing dumb church games, but it ended there.

A few months later, in June 2000, just on my return from a whirlwind European tour of World Cups, I arrived in time to go to the last spiritual retreat of the year. Someone there asked me about my travels and I let out an exhausted sigh. "With the hustle of Europe, all I want to do is spend some time in nature, and if I am really lucky, get in some fishing and golf. And do not even show me a coffee that has less liquid volume than my backwash." Geordie, obviously remembering our last conversation, piped up.

S h e r r a i n e   M a c K a y

"I know how you can accomplish all of those 'goals' in one day with me. Let me pick you up at nine and we'll spend the day together." I shrugged my shoulders and nodded in casual agreement but inside I was bouncing around wide-eyed wanting to tell everyone I saw, "Did you hear that? He asked me out! He asked me out!"

We had an amazing day, starting with a jumbo takeout Second Cup coffee, and drove to his mom's cottage where we caught pathetically small rock bass, hit a few golf balls and thoroughly enjoyed each other's company. From that point on, until I left for the Sydney Olympics in September, we saw each other every single day.

In spite of thinking that it was over before it started, Geordie made it to Paris. In fact, he arrived the same day I did. We were married in July 2001, just over a year after our first date, and within our first month of marriage, we had moved to France together. It was the first time Geordie had ever been to Europe and only the second time he had left North America—the first time happening a few weeks earlier when we went to China for the World University Games—oh, I mean our honeymoon. Marriage had signed Geordie up for many years of exotic travel, thrilling high-level sport and a college student standard of living with no hope for a reasonable pension.

I knew before the Sydney Olympics that I was going to go for Athens 2004, just like I knew going into Athens that I was going to continue until Beijing 2008. I do love teaching, and perhaps people wonder whether I am anxious to get back to Canada to begin my teaching career in earnest. The truth is teaching is very, very secondary. It has always supported my passions: fencing, and most recently, writing. Besides those two things, I am anxious to start a family of my own.

If there is one thing that training for the Olympics taught me, it's that I have married the perfect man. Often people wonder what the spouse of an Olympian must be like ... motivating, disciplined and high achieving? These are all great, but I have found the secret ingredient for those of you who wish to marry an Olympian. You must be cheap. My husband is the cheapest man I know—to such an extreme that when he buys green peppers at the grocery store, he removes their stems to save money when they are weighed. People inevitably ask how I can afford to live making so little money in my low-profile sport. My answer is that marriage was my best money-saving investment. Doubling as my sports agent, Geordie books all my airplane tickets because I can rest easy knowing if anyone can find the cheapest way to get somewhere, he can. (This is the same man who, after seeing the prices of airline tickets to the 2004 Olympics, decided to cycle with his father from our home in Paris all the way to Athens in the August heat.)

His thrift is finely tempered with patience, so he has not become one of those loudly complaining Anglophones that thinks nobody else has to earn a living but him. If, in the middle of shopping in our Paris neighbourhood, he realizes that he has to go to the bathroom, Geordie won't whine about the fact that he has to pay to use a toilet at McDonald's. He will just quietly walk up seven flights of stairs to use the free toilet in our apartment. He is willing to work hard to save money or get a good deal for something, and he is appalled when people waste their money. "Why would you pay one dollar for a bottle of water from a vendor outside of Notre Dame when you could just walk eleven blocks to the supermarket and pay 25 cents!"

Geordie's patience and determination have probably granted him the ability to live with a high-performance athlete and work hard to make the relationship a success. We are not an easy lot. We have high expectations of ourselves, and in stressful times that gets pushed onto others. Geordie is a musician, and when my big competitions would be looming and I was getting a little more stressed every day, I would start to harp on him to practice as much guitar as I did fencing. "Sherraine, I can't spend five to seven hours a day practicing; someone here has to earn a living ... speaking of which, I am almost late for my babysitting job." That's the difficult reality: most Olympic athletes just barely scrape by financially.

Without papers to legally work in France, Geordie's nine to five entails taking care of the apartment and babysitting other people's children. He calls himself a domestic engineer with international investments. In Canada he had a job that he loved: working with adults with disabilities, which required training and certainly delivered job satisfaction. He loved telling me about his clients who would joke at medicine time: "Ahhhh, don't touch my eye with that dropper ... I'll call you 'Popeye'!" Now, in Paris with his babysitting jobs, Geordie is really training to become a parent. The downside is that he is constantly around snivelling kids who have always caught some foreign flu from pawing every surface in the Metro. If this wasn't enough, he could lose his job at any time to a 14-year-old ready to get paid in nachos and ice cream. How many people would willingly pledge their life to someone and agree to stand beside them when they knew that well into their 30s they were going to have to consider a pizza slice and a walk around the neighbourhood "a lovely evening out." When Geordie and I were planning our wedding vows, neither of us bothered to use "for richer or for poorer," because we knew that our standard of living would pretty much stay at the college student level for at least the next decade. And this is his life as he approaches thirty. He swears the payout of spending his days together with me is worth it, but I know I have the better end of the deal. Just don't tell him.

Geordie is an amazing man who knows what is important in life and works everyday to live what he believes. Thankfully, I am important in his life, because I need him. Geordie has a kind innocence that I have never seen in anyone else. In the first month we were living in Paris, we had a fencer—who is from Kuwait but now living in Canada—come and stay with us for a few days. When I came home from practice Geordie was cooking supper for our Kuwaiti friend; he also had asked our two friends from Israel who lived downstairs to come and join them. I walked in and everyone was laughing and having a great time. I knew that it was partly to do with the goodness of our friends but also to do with Geordie's ability to bring people together in a non-threatening atmosphere.

Running With Swords

He had no idea that perhaps there might be tension between people with such different political and religious ideologies because he wasn't really sure what those ideologies were. He just thought that everyone might be hungry and he knew how to cook a good omelette. Geordie is the unknowing master of diplomacy.

Who Here Needs a Pseudonym?

In any career, hobby or workplace there is inevitably some detestable, uncomfortable but necessary task. Mine is fundraising. I have had a love-hate relationship with fundraising since a very young age. On one hand, I love the challenge of selling things to people; on the other hand, I hate seeing people duck around a corner every time I approach them. On one hand, I love the financial reward that comes with sales; on the other hand, I hate the fact that I am usually selling garbage.

In teachers' college we were taught about the human learning process. First, humans learn because they are offered an extrinsic reward: "If you can memorize the alphabet, I will give you a lollipop!" Then it incorporates an understanding of the potential for failure: "If you don't memorize the capital cities of each province, you won't pass the exam!" Finally the last and, in my opinion, most unattainable phase is the completely intrinsic desire to learn: "If you don't learn why Archduke Ferdinand was shot, your life will be that much less fulfilling." Tell that last one to students and you will see 30 pairs of bored eyes. I have discovered that without rewards, humans almost never retain anything. In fact humans don't do much without at least the potential for a reward. Everything from spirituality to school to sports to sales works on this and so has my lifetime battle with fundraising.

In high school, to give the local population reprieve from chocolate-covered almonds, our band sold jewellery just before Christmas. If anyone sold more than 150 items, he or she would receive a CD player. I took the bait. I researched what was the most inexpensive and yet tasteful item in the catalogue and then flogged my wares like Molly Malone in the hallways at each break, lunch, and after school. Unsurprisingly, a CD player was soon delivered to my house over the holiday season and many local women were wearing fake pearl earrings in the New Year. In university things became even more intense as the reward for selling raffle tickets for the sports program was straight up cash. There were a lot of North American Cup tournaments to get to, and I would love to say that people cringed when I came walking over during the tournament because my superior fencing skill intimidated them, but to be honest they were just trying to escape my hard sell.

Selling actual items has never been as bad as having to "sell yourself"—a phrase that has always made me feel shame. When we read *Death of a Salesman* in Grade 11, I felt like someone really understood the discomfort and hesitancy that comes from standing in an office wearing your best Sears catalogue dress clothes, holding your carefully prepared portfolio and waiting to be rejected or rewarded. "Do they want to help me? Do they believe in my cause or do they think that the plight of the amateur athlete has been beaten like a dead horse? Do they think I have asked for too much? Too little? Do I have something in my teeth?" Like Willy Loman from *Death of a Salesman*, fundraising still makes me feel, to this day, "way out there in the blue, riding on a smile and a shoeshine. And when they start not smiling back— that's an earthquake."

I am sure you are hoping that by now in my career things have progressed, especially since I have been ranked in the Top 10 in the world consistently for the past five years. I am sure you are hoping that I no longer have to scrounge and beg for financial support. Well, thanks for your hopes. (You must have also hoped that the Expos would win the World Series?) Here's the real situation. Life is hard, most people are relatively poor and nobody likes to ask for money. We were never a family with a structured cash allowance, but neither do I remember having to constantly ask for money. My parents usually asked my coach for a tentative budget and then made sure I had enough for most of the extra details. They have always been extremely generous with their finances, and best of all, there have never been any strings attached. I never once thought, "Uh-oh, if I spend all their money to go to this competition, Mom and Dad will be really mad if I lose!" It was more along the lines of, "If I spend all this money, I might not have enough to go to the next competition." So aside from buying way too many Guatemalan multi-coloured bracelets, I was usually pretty careful with my money as a teenager.

Recently, when I needed more, I worked, and when I was a little comfortable, I focused more on training. Recently though, I find my parent's continued effort to support me more than a little embarrassing. Just before they left to come and see me compete in Athens 2004, we were talking on the phone and my dad did the typical clearing of his throat. "So how are you for money, anyway?" I smiled, knowing this was German for "I love you" and said, "I am fine dad, I am also 29 and married, but I appreciate the thought. We have enough to get by for now."

All this talk about fundraising is not a whine or an attempt to offer a romantic impression of a starving athlete. I have enough food on my table, and hey—I even have a table; never mind the fact that it is a plastic flip-up, screwed into the wall because my apartment is too small for a permanent table. The only real difficulty comes when I see people my age who have things that are considered "normal," like a house, children, and a bed that you don't have to fold up into your couch every morning. Last Christmas the Canadian Fencing Federation had the brainwave of selling calendars as a fundraiser. I was excited because besides fencing with people, this was finally something I was qualified for! In fact the "work experience" section of my resume reads something like this:

1985-2000 Cocoa-paste-enrobed almond retail supplier
1989-2000 International distributor of casino-selected paper tickets

So now by selling these calendars I could update my resume!
2003-2004 Nation-wide time management advisor

The oil rigs and the cattle slaughtering plant provide the majority of jobs in Brooks, and since women do not have an affinity for working in places where they have to haul two-ton steel pipes or wrap cow's tongues, my hometown has an abnormally high population of young, virile males. While this made life easy for my pretty, 22-year-old friend Amanda Preston selling shots and cigarettes at her summer job at the local bar, it did not help the merchandise turnover for an Olympic athlete and her husband selling sports calendars in the local mall. We sat there, bored and smiling as we sold ... nothing. Our lack of sales was not due to lack of clientele. It was nearly Christmas, and there were lots of people shopping. Of course, most of these people were men slowly walking past checking out my "wares." Geordie and I wondered why nobody seemed too interested until finally one honest young man had the courage and ignorance to tell us why. "Are there pictures of you in a bikini?" motioning to the calendar with a devious, nearly toothless smile.

"No sir, just some great photos of my sport ... fencing!" I responded with Girl Guide enthusiasm.

"Too bad," he drawled as he walked off. "I mighta bought one."

As we realized what most of the world knew already, that sex sells, Geordie flipped madly through the calendar trying to find the month with the most blatantly sexy photo and put it on display. We found one of a woman sabre fencer with her jacket undone ... all the way to her collarbone! Sales picked up a bit after that, but when we realized that we were stealing business from the Boy

Scouts who were selling 50-50 tickets in the mall, we felt kind of bad and so set our sites on Wal-Mart, the Mecca for family Christmas shopping in Brooks. No need for women in bikinis when you're selling to mothers.

Sitting behind a small table still marked with the Scotch tape leftovers from the Mothers Against Drunk Driving display a week before, I tried to convince myself that I was doing something worthwhile. Shouldn't I consider this a public autograph session and thank Les, Wal-Mart's friendly manager, for the free promotion? When one of my high school friends walked in with her two kids, I felt like the character playing the recovering alcoholic in a high school reunion movie. "Oh, wow," she said, "you really kept on with this past high school, eh? Remember when we all used to do it in school? Those were good times but I quit before I became too involved. You really took it all the way, though!"

I kept wondering if anybody else in the Top 10 in the world would be caught dead doing this or if I had truly hit rock bottom. It dawned on me that in many people's opinion, I hadn't really progressed beyond the time when we would sell chocolate bars to raise money for our school band trip. I guess the pay off is different this time: instead of going to Vancouver in a school bus full of band geeks, I would be going to Athens on a plane full of Olympians— as one of the world's elite athletes competing for my country in a sport that I love! After that quick reminder I humbled myself and went back to haranguing each and every Wal-Mart customer to buy my calendar.

Sometimes I find it unsettling to think that my high school friends have their own children, houses, properties, and cars, et cetera. Some of them even have their own rock bands. The chasm between the "haves" and the "have nots" of my generation was made more clear to me in December 2003, when Ryan Vikedal gave me a call out of the blue. "Hey, Sherraine! I'm in Italy right now and I'm calling because we're coming to London really soon and I wanted to know if you and Geordie can come over from Paris to hang out for a few days."

Running With Swords

Ryan was one of my best friends from Grade 7 to 12 when he was the drummer and I played the trumpet in band class. As I did with most of my friends, I convinced him to join the fencing team for a while but soon we all knew that drumming was his destiny. Our paths diverged as we each took the road less travelled. I went to university in Ottawa and studied fencing and literature. He went to Edmonton and studied drumming. I moved to a shoebox-sized apartment in Paris to get better at fencing. Ryan moved to a shoebox-sized apartment in Vancouver to play with better bands. I qualified for the Olympics and was given a free tracksuit from Roots. Ryan joined the band Nickelback which sold over 13 million records, won four Billboard awards, seven Junos and was the first band since the Guess Who to go number one on the charts in both Canada and the USA.

As accomplished as he may be, Ryan has maintained a great attitude, sharing his wealth with friends and family, even now that he is no longer with the band. When he called us to get together in London, we knew he would take good care of us. He offered to let us stay in his hotel room because he knew we couldn't afford to rent one on our own. Since Geordie and I insisted on paying for our own travel, we flew on easyJet, but like most discount airlines, it was anything but easy. We finally found the airport, a pinprick on a national map of France located somewhere between Paris and the English Channel. We made it to London where the city bus dropped us off in a top-notch neighbourhood. We walked around a bit looking for the hotel, and as a last resort I walked into the Hilton where, after sniffing at my jeans and backpack combination, they directed me to the even ritzier hotel across the street, over-looking the gardens of Buckingham Palace. Yes, this is where we would be staying. Geordie and I were giggling as we gave the desk clerk Ryan's pseudonym and she sent us up to his room. Imagine being so famous that you need a pseudonym! The only time I ever try to use another name is when the youth hostel has lost my reservation and I need to take someone else's bunk. We laughed when we went into his ultra-modern fancy room, because while

Ryan and I had both become among the very best in our fields, let's just say that one is an oil field and the other is a cornfield. You know which is which.

Geordie and I were in the catering hall finishing up supper courtesy of Nickelback when their manager came rushing in to get us. "Ryan needs you both upstairs right away for their pre-concert shot!" Now, I have experienced two types of pre-performance "shots." I was suffering from terrible tennis elbow and the team doctor gave me multiple shots of painkiller to get me through my last and most important day of the season. The only other "shot" I have experienced before a performance is when our national coach took a group photo of us to give to Prieur, our equipment sponsors at the time. Seeing as this pre-concert shot seemed to involve a lot of people I knew it couldn't be an injection of painkiller, so I assumed this was a traditional group photo. I was excited; what a great memory! Well, as it turns out, it wasn't a memory I could paste in my photo album, because the pre-concert shot was a shot of whisky. Musicians might claim that their bodies are essential keys to their greatness, but let me assure you that if I took a shot of whisky before I tried to wield a sword it would prove very difficult. Athletes keep their bodies in pristine shape for competitions so they can chase after a golden medal. Rock stars use a chaser of golden liquid to be in fine shape for their shows.

The concert was amazing. Truly the best rock show I have ever attended. Because I am always eager to improve fencing's appeal to spectators and make it more popular, I watched their performance carefully hoping to use rock show tactics to making fencing competitions more interesting. I had already considered the dramatic surge in beach volleyball's popularity but decided that while fencing in bikinis would definitely draw crowds, it would also draw blood. Unfortunately, Nickelback's concert devices were completely inappropriate in the fencing world. Fencing has a long-standing tradition of honourable and sportsmanlike behaviour, probably due to its glorious (and very distant) past as the chosen method of duelling. Referees have the power to punish a fencer for unsporting behaviour by either giving a point to the opponent or by removing the offender from the bout entirely. For example, every time a fencer curses, the judge can award a point to the opponent or even expel that person from the match; so Chad, the lead singer, would be in the negatives after about a minute—and gone in the next. Second, if a fencer commits a violent act, such as throwing her mask, she is "black-carded," which removes her from the competition—in fact, the fencer is also instructed to leave the venue immediately. So Ryan, who insists that the crowd loves it when he hurls his drumsticks at them, would be immediately ejected from the premises. Mike, the bassist, would be sent packing for "delay of game" as there are strict rules about the number of times you can stop to change your épée in a match. The man uses no fewer than eight bass guitars for a two-hour concert. Eight! Finally, although the International Fencing Federation has not yet been forced to create this rule, I am sure that the lead guitarist, Ryan Peake, would promptly be black-carded for throwing full cups of beer into the cheering crowd.

After the two nights of rock shows ended, it was time for the band to get into their luxury tour buses and move on to Manchester. Suddenly, Ryan realized something: Geordie and I weren't leaving London until the next day. "Hey, you guys can totally keep the room that I stayed in and I'll just pay for you!"

I looked at Geordie who had almost let the "Sure!" escape his lips before I stomped on his toe.

"No, we're fine," I said too quickly. "We'll just stay in a hostel or a cheap hotel or something. Your hotel is like five hundred pounds a night; Geordie and I don't need that." It was the response of a proud woman who ought to have shut her big, fat mouth. "Okay," Ryan said slowly, probably wondering what the inside of a hostel looked like, "but only if you're sure you'll be okay, because another night of hotel is really no problem."

We assured Ryan that he had already helped us more than enough and said our goodbyes.

"See you next time you're in Europe. Say 'Hi' to your mom, and thanks again for the drumsticks," I said.

When we finally arrived at our hostel we knew we had made a mistake. We would contract fewer diseases sleeping in a dung pile, but at one in the morning there was no where else to go. The concierge pushed a rat off of his chair, which fell with a thud before scampering off, and then he sat down to serve us.

"What can I help you with?" he asked in a tired English accent.

"We reserved a room. MacKay."

He ran his overgrown, yellowed fingernails over the list of guests, "Nope," he said, "you guys reserved beds."
"Sure, whatever." At this point I thought all I wanted was a bed. We took the key and went up to our room. Even though it was winter, Geordie refused to wear any sort of gloves, so I put myself in charge of touching things like keys and door handles. When I opened the door to our room we were hit with the pungent smell of underhanded deeds. Literally. Under the buzz of fluorescent lights my eyes were drawn to the only person in the room. He was tucked into his bed, watching television and sweating.

Hoping that Geordie had not seen enough to have the image burned into his mind forever, I quickly made an executive decision. "Goodbye," I said as we backed out of the room and closed the door behind us.

We returned to our jaundiced friend, the desk clerk, and he sullenly booked us into a private room, which for only 20 pounds more was guaranteed to be as filthy, but at least it would be our own for the next few hours. I walked into the room, took off my coat and placed it on the only piece of furniture, a scratched-up wooden chair. My shoes I wore until I carefully, without touching any surface but the sheets (which were probably the only things that had been washed since the seventies), stepped into the bed where I lay, unmoving, until morning. I had the whole night to think about how different my life would be if I were talented at beating an instrument with sticks instead of poking people with them.

Running With Swords

I don't know what I was thinking as I woke up the next morning and went down to the first floor for the "included breakfast." Perhaps because the sun was shining, I thought, "Come on Sherraine, last night couldn't have been so bad ... it probably wasn't even real. Just sit down and enjoy some good English breakfast." As we walked into the tattered breakfast room, there, strewn about, was a refrigerator, some folding wooden chairs, a tub of crumb-filled margarine, a bag of Wonder bread, a couple of butter knives and two people. One was a white-haired woman who looked from me to Geordie with blissful recognition.

"Oh, hello!"

I looked at Geordie. Did he know her? He gave me a quick shake of his head.

"Hello?" I offered. She kept beaming at us so I turned to look at our other breakfast companion. In case I might not have recognized him from last night, he gave me a guilty, sheepish look and I knew right away. Another executive decision was made. "Goodbye," I said, and we slowly backed out of the room and onto the street.

A few months after that I received an e-mail from Ryan, who was still on tour:

> *I stayed at this hotel in Denmark the other day and the reception lady was freaking out because Paul McCartney left just before we got there. I had one room and he had the whole second floor. CRAZY, eh?*

It sure is.

THE LANGUAGE of LOVE

When Geordie and I moved to Paris in September 2001 to train for the 2004 Athens Olympics, we knew we would be making some sacrifices. The first thing to be sacrificed was our dignity. The stories that you hear of the French waiters and shopkeepers making fun of English speakers for bastardizing the language of love are absolutely untrue. A French stranger will never make fun of you, only your French friends will. And they won't even correct your grammar, just the accent. Your basic understanding of the language could be completely off but all they will say is, "No, no, no, you've got it all wrong. It is not 'I seeing the cinema at the movie last week,' it is '*ci*nema,' d'accord?" What the French don't realize is that we only put our lips in kissing position to form three letters: *o*, *q* and *u*. Parisians pride themselves on speaking as though at any time someone is going to walk up and plant one on them, and boy, they had better be ready!

Daniel Levavasseur had been my coach since September 2001, when I decided I had to spar with the very best in Paris. That's when I left my old coach, Jean Michel, who lived in Bordeaux. Daniel knew that I would need something to do besides fencing

R u n n i n g   W i t h   S w o r d s

full-time, and all the better if it earned me a little money. So he found me a job as an English teacher at INSEP (the National Institute for Sport and Physical Studies), France's training centre for almost all of its summer Olympic sports. My students were all high-level athletes and coaches. The same system applies to both teachers and students: if you have a training camp or competition, all classes are cancelled, no questions asked. My students were very understanding about my training schedule (all our classes had to be during the day), but likewise, I have had to be even more understanding, because when they would go away to Guadeloupe for a two-week training camp, I was two weeks without income!

My students spend their day giving their bodies a workout and then they come to English class to give their lips a workout. This was a perfect job for me, as I was a fresh graduate of Teachers' College (in spring 2001). My dad helped me make up my mind in spring 2000 to do a teaching degree because teaching jobs would be among the ones I would most likely get in Europe while training and competing, and it's a fine career path to fall back on. I tried to explain to my students that in English we use our tongue to form our words, not our lips. Then I get to watch as they laboriously pronounce words like "three thousand three hundred and thirty three," all the while wondering why anyone would ever think to call it "French" kissing.

My students at INSEP all came to me wanting to learn English but for very different reasons. My favourite student was a judo champion named Jerome Dreyfuss. He was a stereotypical case of the bigger the man, the softer the heart. He was taking English classes to better converse with his in-laws from Manchester. As well as making me feel tiny for the first time in my life, being his teacher made me mentally stronger. He was such a natural coach—which he has since become—that our lessons were like sports psychology sessions in which he encouraged, reproved and analyzed my training.

Teaching at INSEP was quite different from my first job teaching at a private French high school. You are probably thinking it must have been easy with all the rich, overachieving Parisians eager to learn English for their trips around the world, but in France, "private schools" are often reserved for those students who have failed too many times to stay in the regular system. So, lucky me, I was teaching students up to 21 years of age who just couldn't learn enough to pass their exams. Regardless, it was a good experience and it fine-tuned my French. Nothing is more embarrassing than lecturing a class and watching them restrain themselves from correcting your mistakes: "You are making really my day going bad, so you better listening!"

The most embarrassing moments didn't come from my bad grammar, however, but from lack of familiarity with cultural innuendo. On my first day of teaching I was hesitating between introducing myself as "Mrs. MacKay" or just "Sherraine." I eventually ended up going with the old Madame route, hoping it would establish some modicum of respect early on. Nice thought.

"Bonjour, class! My name is Madame MacKay." I knew they were high school students but I half expected the sing-song, "Bonjour Madame MacKay!"

All I heard was giggling. One boy raised his hand. "Can we just call you MacKay?" he asked.

"No, you can call me Mrs. or Madame MacKay." I shook my head in confusion and we carried on with class.

This happened every time I introduced myself to a class. Finally I asked one of the other English teachers to explain this odd behaviour. "Oh, you pronounce your name 'Ma-Kai,' like rhyming with 'bye'?" she asked.

"Yeah, it's something to do with two Scottish brothers who came to Canada, began fighting among themselves and instead of one changing his name he changed the pronunciation to 'MacKay,'" I explained. She smiled. "When you pronounce your name like that in French it sounds exactly like an expression of endearment that men use for their wives. It literally means 'My quail' but it can be translated to something like 'darling' or 'honey.'"

So much for formality; so much for respect.

I don't know who had it worse, Geordie or I. Geordie's comprehension was weaker, but he had a far better accent, so there were fewer people making fun of him. But that didn't let him get away without embarrassing moments. The very first time he came to watch one of my practices I was getting a lesson from my coach, Daniel. Part of the French system of improvement is to tell you how terrible you are to make you want to work even harder. Daniel was trying to improve my speed, so there I was, puffing like mad trying to keep up with him as he told me that I looked like a grandma. Most of the time, I just stopped listening. During one of my rare rest moments he looked over at Geordie and said in French, "She is a grandma, eh?" I heard that one and slowly turned my head but I already knew inside that Geordie would be insulted on my behalf and probably roll his eyes or shake his head in disapproval at Daniel's comment. When I turned to see Geordie giving a big, toothy smile and a double thumbs up in response I seethed. After my lesson I went and sat down beside him. "What were you thinking agreeing with that garbage?"

"What?" Geordie looked confused.

"When Daniel said, 'She is a grandma?' Do you really think that you married a grandma?"

He gulped. "You mean he didn't say, 'She is beautiful?'"

"You expect me to believe that you heard 'Elle est belle' instead of 'Elle est une *grandmere*'?"

"Grand-*mere* means grandma?" he asked innocently.

"One 'Get Out Of Jail Free' mister, but no more excuses for that one!" and I went to finish up my practice.

If it started off badly, at least Geordie's French improved over the years we lived in Paris. I could not say the same for Daniel's English. If you ever ask Daniel if there's anything he *can't* do, he will respond with a wholehearted, "Of course not! I can do anything!"

Ask him the same question in English and you will get a blank stare followed by a dopey smile as he waits for you to translate the question into French. The man honestly cannot learn English. I know. I was, for a brief moment, his English teacher.

Our lessons started with what I thought he would need to know. He is a pretty sociable guy, so we started with pleasantries. Having travelled to the USA, Canada, England, Australia and New Zealand many times over the past 20 years, I thought he would have picked up some of the basics: "Hello, how are you, my name is …"—that sort of thing. Thankfully, he had learned something by osmosis. His responses were generic. "Hello" was his only greeting, and I guess Anglophone countries put him in a good mood because he was always "Fine, sank you. And you?" I wanted him to feel comfortable speaking, even if he was going to make some errors at first, so I was quite encouraging. "You're doing well! Good response, Daniel! When you say, 'I speak very well English,' it shows you are positive about your learning! Excellent vocabulary, there, Daniel; 'Rocker-man' is a rarely used word since Freddie Mercury died!" I had an underhanded intention with our lessons. I hoped that my encouragement would make him appreciate the value of positive feedback, and perhaps lead him to offer some in our fencing lessons to keep my morale afloat. After a few English lessons, he sat me down and told me that I was way too nice and gave way too much encouragement. If I wanted him to improve, I would have to be meaner, make fun of him more and make him see just how bad he was. I nodded and realized that not only had my plan failed, but I was doomed to this treatment for the next few years.

There was one moment when I agreed that I should have been tougher on him, because he made absolutely no effort to learn real words. He just tried to remember more or less how they sounded and hoped that his charm would fill in the gaps. This was painfully obvious when we were in Brazil at a training camp. He was lecturing South American coaches on coaching and at one point he wanted to get Monique's and my attention. (Monique Kavelaars is a good friend, and because she's a teammate I get to travel the world with her. Travelling with her has eliminated my need to buy a Game Boy. She's like a living pinball machine: she can quiet down, but usually only when there is no one else around. Otherwise she is all lights, bells and non-stop action. We really became friends when she and I were on the national team in 1999 and she moved in right across the hall from me to train in Paris in 2002 (about six months after I did). She and I helped each other deal with the cultural alienation and language barriers we often experienced. She made the national team again in 2003 and went to Olympics with me in 2004. Our friendship is based on mutual respect, similar interests and plain old laughter.) Daniel must have thought the other coaches would be impressed if they heard him speaking English to his two new students, because he whirled around to where we were talking and boomed, "Monique, Sherraine, look my eggs!" As he expressed this absurdly bizarre directive he pointed with two fingers at his eyeballs. "Look my eggs!" he repeated. A few of the coaches who understood English started snickering. I couldn't let this go on; the man had to maintain some dignity.

"Eggs? Those are 'eyes,' coach!"

As ungifted as he may be for languages, Daniel definitely has a gift for laughing at himself, which is one of his best qualities. He was cracking up for days about the eggs. While he still laughs at that today, I can guarantee that if you ask him what the English word is for those two small balls located above your nose, Daniel would give you a blank stare followed by a dopey smile and then wait for the French translation.

Life in the French Lane

The hardest thing about having an income below the Canadian poverty line is that I live in Paris. I can't complain too much, though. Since the Revolution, the French government has been pretty careful about maintaining a support system for the underprivileged. As Geordie and I fall into that category because we earn less in a month than some people spend on freshly cut flowers, we get inexpensive but quality health care and the occasional rent supplement. And in Paris, if you're really down and out and can't seem to find another way to work the system, you can storm the mayor's office and beg for money. That was advice given to me from the National Gas and Electricity representative when I went to see how we could cut back on our energy consumption. Apparently, if things aren't going well, you can just go to your neighbourhood mayor (they have 20 "arrondissement" mayors in Paris) and ask the big guy for a handout. Often it works. It is a shame that I learned this only a few days before I left for the Olympics because I would have loved to have done it, if only for the story I could tell at dinner parties.

In France, nobody talks about money. If you're rich, you don't want to brag by talking about money, and if you are poor, that's between you and the mayor. I imagined all the self-righteous capitalists in my hometown leaning in as I told them that in the magical land of France, when I needed a little extra cash I didn't have to work hard to get it. Instead of letting the Invisible Hand guide my financial progression, I just walked over to the mayor's office and he wrote me a cheque. They would gasp at the injustice of it all. How the French taxpayers must be furious, they'd say. But since they weren't paying French taxes, deep down I am sure they would be completely jealous.

Geordie and I referred to our first home as the "Tip o' the Tower" because if you managed to climb the 150 steps to get to our apartment and went out onto the tiny balcony, you were rewarded with a distant view of the very tip of the Eiffel Tower. I know it sounds enchanting, and with the thin air and the lack of oxygen to your brain at this height, sometimes it was. (Paris is much more charming if you are too far up to smell the dog poo.) The apartment came "furnished," which meant that we paid cash to the former tenant to leave us her fridge and stove. She threw in two electric heaters for free, so our 180-foot palace was warm and cozy. As small as it was, we never took our apartment for granted because I can tell you that it is easier to get a painting hung on the walls of the Louvre than to rent an apartment in Paris. When I came here looking for a place to live, I experienced my first cultural rejection. Because I was a Canadian, nobody wanted to rent to me. "Do you earn more than three times the rent of this apartment? Do you know a taxpaying French citizen who is willing to vouch for you in writing, providing their bank account number to be charged on your behalf in case you fail to pay your rent? Do you know how lucky you are to even be walking on our beautiful streets?" These were all questions I was asked by housing agents through a haze of cigarette smoke. After weeks of this fruitless searching, I walked into "The Moose," a Canadian bar and restaurant in Paris. I went straight up to the bartender and actually slammed my fist on the bar. "Please tell me that you know someone who wants to rent an apartment to a Canadian."

Shocked and probably a little frightened, Mark the bartender said, "Strangely enough, I do." He seemed as surprised at his response as I was. "She should be here any minute now." Apparently one of his friends was leaving Paris and her apartment would be free in a couple of weeks. In the end it was too expensive for us to stay longer than a few months and after promising to give our firstborn child to our new landlord, we were granted permission to rent the "Tip o' the Tower." The building was horribly run down but we didn't mind the cracks in the walls and even the crack of our neighbour who occasionally danced around naked in front of his window, blasting techno music. This glorious place was ours as long as we paid rent ... and even if we didn't. French law forbids landlords to evict their tenants between the months of October and April because doing so in the 10-degree winter temperature is considered cruel. As Canadians, we knew that cruelty starts at minus 40 Celsius, and if you have your Kodiak boots on, you're okay for another 10-degree drop ... but we paid our rent anyway.

I am not sure what "rent" covers outside of permission to sleep behind your own door, because in Paris, if anything goes wrong in the apartment, it is completely the tenant's responsibility. From changing hot water tanks to introducing the concept of fire alarms, we were truly in charge of the place. Last year, my brother Sherwin, self-styled "Captain of All Home Security," finally decided to visit Europe. He made his first-ever European trip to visit my sister Jonene and her husband, Jeff Shantz, who were living in Switzerland after Jeff signed with the Langnau Tigers, a Swiss pro hockey team. So Sherwin's introduction to Europe was the very structured, very safe and very calm Switzerland. Entering our apartment in Paris, he realized he had seen no fire alarms on any landings and that if something started burning on the lower floors, we would be eating cheese and baguettes and watching dubbed reruns of *MacGyver* until the flames were licking at our door.

Sherwin solved our safety issues the next morning en route to the Eiffel Tower. He took us to a hardware store where he bought us our first fire extinguisher. When he asked the salesman about fire alarms, he was shocked to learn that they are only available at specialty shops way outside of central Paris. Then it dawned on me that I couldn't remember ever seeing a fire alarm in Paris, and my theory is that the French are afraid that their continual cigarette smoking will set off the alarm. "Why would I want zis screeching noise to 'appen non-stop, chez moi?" During Christmas in Brooks a month later, my brother slid a present over to me, which judging by its bulky shape, was not the new U2 CD. Inside was a 100-foot rope for rappelling down the side of the building and a matching set of smoke alarms.

One irony here is that while the country as a whole is well known for its many large-scale acts of kindness, Parisians themselves are not accustomed to performing individual or spontaneous acts of kindness. Doctors Without Borders and the Red Cross are two of many examples that prove that the country has a big heart. However, it is no coincidence that those groups of kind, giving people have all left France, working their good deeds abroad. What we have left in Paris are the takers. But like most generalizations, as soon as you have something firmly developed, there is an exception that comes along to dash your stereotype. One winter morning I was rushing off to teach English on the other side of the city. I looked at my watch and realized that I would be late if I didn't catch the very next train, so I ran out onto the platform just as the buzzer was sounding, signalling the automatic closing of the doors. When these doors shut, they shut. There are stickers on the inside of the car that show a pink cartoon rabbit looking surprised with his little fingers caught in the sliding doors, and the sign says in four languages, "Beware: when buzzer sounds, doors are closing." I'd watched plenty of women getting their purses squashed flat and girls with their backpacks hanging outside the doors as they stand waving their arms like a trapped bug.

Well, that morning I'd jumped inside just in time. I let out a big sigh of relief, and as expected, such an outward expression of my thoughts drew every pair of eyes. (If you want to fit into the French Metro culture, you have to keep the same expressionless face at all times, without exception. Bomb threats, drunks urinating on themselves, really bad accordion players: these are all met with the same dignified air of indifference.) Seconds after looking at me, all eyes were diverted to a man running on the platform alongside the train. He ran up beside our car and threw something through the tiny window and onto a woman's lap. She was as surprised as anyone and let out a yelp. As I regarded her with a sharp glare to remind her to please maintain a proper French dignity, thank you very much, I noticed that she was holding something familiar. It was my scarf. Confused, I blurted out, "Hey, that's my scarf!" The woman shrugged and held it out for me. As I walked over to get it, lurching with the movement of the train, it dawned on me that the man must have seen me drop my scarf on the platform as I ran to catch the Metro. He'd run like a madman to give it back. Such a kind effort put a big, goofy smile on my face. When I looked up, I was shocked to find that the cool expressions on everyone's face had melted: every single person on the car was smiling! Outside of winning a soccer match against the English, it is rare to see a whole Metro car full of smiling faces, and I felt proud to be a part of such a gracious moment.

If there is one thing besides soccer that makes the French smile, it is Michael Moore's movies. They love anything that shows Americans in a bad light. Sometimes I panic, thinking they will assume that I am American and will treat me with disdain, but the French really pride themselves on being able to tell the difference between Americans and Canadians. Surprisingly, even an English-speaking Canadian like me who insists on carrying a Starbucks thermal coffee mug around the streets of Paris is rarely mistaken for an American by the discerning French. They know more about Canada than most people from Europe ... although to be completely honest, their knowledge tends to be limited to French-speaking areas. "Oh, you're from Canada! Montreal? Non? Quebec? Non?"

The revolutionary French do love to associate Canada with our submission to Her Majesty, the Queen. One time, Her Royal Highness was visiting Paris, paying her diplomatic respects to the French president and the mayor, having short coffees instead of high tea. The hoopla surrounding her visit didn't concern me very much; it's not like I was going to run into her. I don't frequent the Champs-Elysées, and the chances of me meeting her on the Metro were slim, so I didn't think much of Queen Elizabeth's visit ... until I went to physiotherapy.

I had been going to physiotherapy at my training centre, the Racing Club, several times per week during that month to take care of some tendonitis located where my buttock meets my leg, in between my groin and hamstring, an unfortunate spot both for me and my shy physiotherapist. Laurent tried his utmost to be discreet as he rubbed ultrasound gel into my nether regions, and to avoid any sort of uncomfortable silences we usually chatted about anything and everything. The other day, our chat was cut short by incessant honking on the street outside of the training club. I looked up from the medical table to see a policeman blocking off traffic. He stood in front of the line of cars imploring them to quiet down by frantically putting his finger to his lips in a shushing motion and waving his hands down to sign for an end to the clamour.

"Ah, ha!" Laurent said. "It's *your* queen in town causing all the chaos! She's going to drive by in a minute and that's why they are stopping traffic."

Sensing his condescending, republican attitude, I responded as best I could, "Oh come on, she is not really *our* queen ... I've always thought the monarchy to be a stupid tradition that only wastes taxpayer's money. I don't even know why we are still a part of this supposed 'commonwealth.' The wealth certainly doesn't feel very common ..."

To keep the discussion going, Laurent suddenly took the other viewpoint, "But Sherraine, she doesn't use *that* much money, and it is nice to keep that tradition alive. It gives a certain stability to a culture and you shouldn't lose that," he reasoned.

And this from a Frenchman whose forefathers stormed the Bastille and guillotined their royalty? I've often found that knowing a people's history doesn't prepare you for the subtleties of the culture that it produces.

"Still," I said, hanging on to my position, "I don't see what the big deal is about her … I mean, she's just a regular woman."

"Well your regular woman should be driving by any time now in a Bentley," Laurent chided. "Of course we won't see her as the windows will certainly be tinted."

Sure enough, a few seconds later while I was lying bare-bummed on the physio table looking out the third floor window of 5 rue Eble, I glanced up just in time to see a Bentley gliding by with Queen Elizabeth inside, waving to her adoring public. She didn't even have tinted windows, although with her intense lime green dress she really should have considered it.

In a rare moment, I was struck dumb as we watched her pass by, and as much to my surprise as anyone's, I turned around giggling and blushing, stuttering, "Laurent, I saw the queen! I really saw the Queen!" After all of my nonchalance, I turned out to be as big a sucker as anyone when it comes to royalty. As much as I hate being pegged a certain way, if the worst thing that the French can come up with for a generalization about Canadians is that we are royalists, we aren't too badly off. Just ask Michael Moore.

Lex LutHor Wins Olympic Games

Will it all be worth it? Can I really make this work? Am I supposed to be here, or have I made a horrible mistake and now it's too late to go back? You might expect these questions to be asked by those poor stressed-out astronauts in Apollo 13, or the people aboard the HMS *Titanic*, and possibly even a groom the night before his marriage, but would you expect a heavily favoured Olympic athlete to be asking those questions at the start of the final World Cup season before the Games?

I had won World Cups in Austria in 2003, Cuba and Puerto Rico in 2002, and also in Spain in 2000. I had medalled at 12 other World Cups. I had been ranked as high as second in the world. My physique had improved dramatically, my footwork was far better, and I had expanded my range of techniques and tactics greatly. Since that win in Cuba, I had been able to win bouts against several different styles, and I was now on par with the very best fencers in the world. And yet there I was with those same uncertainties running through my head as I discussed my goals for the upcoming year with my husband. Of course my coach had influenced my goal setting also. He thought I should aim to finish number one overall and win a gold medal at the Olympics. His philosophy was that at my level one should prepare to win every competition, or else why bother entering the competition at all? My list of goals was pretty hefty and, in retrospect, they were too many and unrealistic, which led to the self-doubt. Challenging goals are important, but I became lost wanting to be the best in everything and everywhere. Allow me to share my pre-season goals, and you can be the judge.

Goal number one: To help qualify the Canadian Women's Épée Team Canada for the Athens Olympics

Goal number two: To win every World Cup I attend

Goal number three: To be ranked number one overall going into the Olympics

Goal number four: To win the Olympics

Goal number five: To win the lottery

Okay, maybe number five was wishful thinking considering I forgot to buy a ticket, but the rest of them seemed very reasonable at the time. Nowhere in there did I list, "To have a deeper under-standing of humility." Nor did I mention, "To learn to pursue excellence in spite of failure" or "To realize that my identity is not defined by my accomplishments." These were the goals that I actually accomplished, outside of number one. I guess if you have the foresight to make those types of "make you a better person" goals instead of "world domination" goals, you probably don't need the harsh lessons that I learned from trying to meet the ones I first picked. Obviously these weren't set with any sort of professional trainer or I would have been stopped as soon as I said the word "every." I just formed my goals from what I knew of the successful career pattern of the athlete I respect the most: Catriona Le May Doan. She has won practically everything she was expected to, and also wins when she is not expected to. My understanding of race sports is limited, never mind those done on ice, but I have always been amazed at athletes like Catriona who win under pressure. So I set my goals accordingly. And wrongly.

The bad thing about making goals that use the words "win"

and "everything" is that deep down you know it's impossible, so you don't take your goal-setting very seriously. Then you can't distinguish the real ambitions from those that you made just to sound powerful. I have since realized that goals must be brief, challenging, but humanly possible. Forget world domination; I'll leave that to Lex Luthor. I just want to win the Olympics some day. Is that too much to ask?

These are all things that I have learned over this past year. For the time being, I had a whole season of World Cups ahead of me and a desire to really dominate the women's épée circuit. With those fatal objectives in mind, I set out into my final World Cup season before the Athens Olympics.

Göteborg, Sweden.
January 12–13, 2004

T he year started with a bang. This was the first World Cup of the season and it felt like a homecoming as we flew from grey, dusty and mild Paris to sunny, snowy and cold Göteborg, Sweden.

With all the international travel we do, waiting at airports has become a standard and boring part of our lives, a lot like waiting at bus stops. While some people are thinking, "Why is the number 96 always late?" we are asking ourselves, "Why do we always fly Air France?" Prior to take off, Monique presented an idea to the rest of us girls on the Canadian National team: Marie-Eve Pelletier, Julie Leprohon, Catherine Dunnette and me. Hearing Moe's crazy idea reminded us that in her hometown of Appin, Ontario, which was small enough to warrant only a single traffic light, she obviously grew up creating her own fun out of nothing. She said that since it was the start of the World Cup season and we had tons of travelling to do, we should develop some sort of betting system and turn travelling the World Cup circuit into a casino. Yes, we were desperate. But try hauling a 70-pound fencing bag around Europe and you will understand why we were anxious for a distraction. Monique's future husband plays professional hockey, and she'd gotten this idea from him. We had already heard their stories of putting shaving cream on fresh towels and snapping backsides with wet ones, so we were wary of this big idea, except for Julie, whose boyfriend also plays semi-pro hockey, so she seemed willing to hear Moe out. Moe smiled and took centre stage: "It's easy. We make a betting pool and each time we take an airplane everyone puts in a Euro —"

"Whoa!" Julie said. "Betting money? Money I could lose? A Euro is a Euro! Money is not something to be throwing away, girls!" Julie studies commerce at McGill.

"Well we should at least hear her out, Julie. It sounds like a good chance to win something." Catherine Dunnette has three sisters and has spent her life competing with them in everything from potty training to school grades.

Monique continued, "So, as I was saying, at the end of every flight as our bags come down the carousel, we see whose bag arrives first, and they win the pot of Euros for that trip."

Monique knew she could count on me to participate. She remembered the story of me eating a worm gizzard in high school biology class for the low, low price of twenty bucks. "You mean we don't have to eat anything disgusting?"

"Nope."

"Well then I'm in," I said.

After much deliberation over whether a Euro was a small enough amount to be betting, we all agreed to this new game and boarded the plane.

To add to the excitement we decided to name our bags. It's pretty obvious that we are all women who do not yet have children, because we still love naming things. Monique's sturdy bag was christened "Big Red." Mine was skinny and looked like it had lived through the worst of the '70s, so I called it "Purple Haze." Marie-Eve's (we call her M'eve) was "Koala," after its dull, grey colour and because of her fascination with the cuddly bears. Catherine's overweight beast was named "Bertha Blue" and Julie, whose creative juices were surging that day, named her burgundy-coloured bag "Burgundy."

So there we were at the airport in Göteborg, shaking with excitement over whose bag would come rolling down the chute first. We were standing at the baggage carousel like five-year-olds looking up the chimney for Santa. Finally I saw Marie-Eve smile in quiet contentment. Koala had won the season opener. We all handed over our Euros, except Catherine, who always seemed to be slow coughing up. "And if there is one person who never wins? What happens to that person? This could be very risky!" Julie's reservations had resurfaced as she gave away her Euro coin. We assured her that it was practically impossible for one person to lose all the time and that she would certainly have her winning day. In retrospect, we shouldn't have been so certain.

After losing the first four bag bets, Julie took drastic measures. She changed her bag's name from just plain "Burgundy" to "Lucky Burgundy," telling us that she just wanted to encourage him to perform. She could have named him "Horseshoe Rabbit's Foot" but it still wouldn't have made him any luckier. He didn't win until the first time we agreed not to play anymore, and for a while after that he was always arriving in the lead.

Just past noon the sun was already starting to set, leaving us to muddle our way toward the youth hostel in near darkness. Control freak that I am, I had written down exact directions from the airport to the youth hostel and from the hostel to the competition. I blamed my lack of concentration on the cold, as I misread my own instructions and led my four teammates, most of whom had travelled all the way from Canada that same day, 45 minutes away from the hostel and into a village of Volvo dealerships. Frustrated, we hauled our huge fencing bags off the tram and changed directions. When the ticket controllers showed up to verify that we had paid the proper amount to be travelling such a distance, they gave us a break when we said we were new to the country and that the cold had frozen our brains. They let us stay on and only made us re-punch our tram cards. I had actually led my naive teammates outside of the city limits! Luckily, this was Sweden and not France, where they would have fined us on the spot.

After a fitful sleep, we rose with the sun at about 8.30 a.m. After a few tram transfers, we arrived at the competition shivering, where only 69 girls were registered to fence. Normally a competition has at least a hundred, so this was a rarity. Since I am in the top 16 in the world, I don't have to fence in the qualification rounds on the first day, so I went back to the youth hostel and began to focus on the competition. The other girls arrived back at about 6:00 p.m. full of excitement because they had all qualified for the next day. For that, we needed a big meal, but because of the outrageous costs of restaurants in Sweden we just went to the grocery store and picked up frozen TV dinners. The youth hostel where we were staying had cooking facilities and in seven minutes we had our supper of champions.

The competition started at 9 a.m. the next morning, so we arrived at about 7:30 only to find several other eager fencers shivering in front of the locked doors to the venue. I volunteered to run around to the other entrances and find an open door. When I found some cleaning ladies, I realized that even if I wanted to, I couldn't ask them to open the front doors because the only Swedish words I could speak were the "boork, boork" sounds I learned from the Swedish Chef on the Muppet Show. So I jogged all the way back to the front doors and guided the others to the open doors in the back of the building. I considered this an early-bird warm-up for the competition, but it proved unnecessary because the low attendance and my high ranking gave me a bye in the first round of 64, so I didn't have my first match until 11:00 a.m.!

My first match was against a Greek girl, Gianna Christou, and it was close, going into sudden-death overtime. Just before the overtime, Charis Tsolakis, the Greek coach, came up and gave her advice. Now a few months ago, Charis and I were talking about how difficult it was to get accommodations for people coming to the Olympics. My parents, my sister and her husband and their two children, and my husband and his parents and his sister were are all planning on attending the Games, so I was trying to find an inexpensive hotel for them. After much discussion, Charis had finally come up to me at a competition and said, "Listen, Sherraine, I am sorry, but finding accommodation is going to be next to impossible, so if they want, they can stay at my apartment." I was shocked and couldn't stop thanking him for his thoughtfulness. We talked about the logistics and made plans for August. So here I was, tied with his athlete and going into overtime, and a thought flashed through my head: if I beat her, will he "forget" his offer? Then where would the whole clan stay? In spite of this worry an overwhelming *need* to win came over me and I thought, who cares! My parents are used to camping; they can bloody well bring a tent to the Olympics! And I landed the last hit.

My next match was against an Australian lawyer named Evelyn Halls. Twenty-eight hits later we were tied at 14–14 in overtime. I finished her off with a final hit to the shoulder. Moving into the quarter-finals, I came up against another lawyer: Hungarian Ildiko Minzca-Nebald. She is one of the most consistent performers on the circuit. Fortunately, I fared pretty well against her and I won 15–10. At one point in our match, my épée suddenly didn't work and instead of immediately handing it to the judge, I did a no-no and tested it myself. However, the judge didn't see me test it, so when I presented it to him and he proved that indeed it didn't work, he annulled Ildiko's point. Imagining how frustrating that would be if it had happened to me, I quickly admitted that I had committed a fault and gave her the point. She extended her hand and we shook as she thanked me for my fair play, and I said, "You're welcome. I know you would do the same thing." And trust me, Ildiko would.

From there it was into the top three where I met Britta Heidemann, who we have nicknamed "The Gentle Giant" because of her height and personality. She fences like she would rip your head off and then chase your headless, quivering body across the gym through a shower of your gushing blood. As soon as the match is over, she becomes her usual kind self and sincerely apologizes

Running With Swords

for any harm that she may have inflicted upon you in the course of the match. Instead of the typical "YAAAH!" scream that high-level fencers seem to be required to develop, Britta has a sort of diabolical laugh which erupts every time she scores a critical point. Well, 15 diabolical laughs later, I had to settle for third place even though our match was a lot of fun and exciting for the crowd. As the President of the Swedish Fencing Federation was shaking my hand on the podium and awarding me a lovely set of candlesticks as a prize, he whispered in my ear, "I wish that you had won—you were my favourite to watch!" I blushed and said, "I bet you say that to all the girls." Fortunately, as he started to reminisce about his good old partying days with the president of the Canadian Fencing Federation, the Hungarian national anthem started to play in tribute to Adrienne Hormay, who had beaten Britta in the final, so I never heard just how much vodka was consumed.

Budapest, Hungary.
January 23–26, 2004

With only a week in between competitions, and knowing that we were going back home to Paris for a few short days, we didn't even unpack our bags. We just refilled the shampoo bottles and looked forward to Budapest. We arrived at the Charles De Gaulle Airport in Paris two-and-a-half hours before takeoff, not to hear Monique's new plan for fun but to calm down our coach. He has an insatiable need to arrive earlier than everyone else for everything. This has led to hours spent in duty-free shops and many early mornings spent shivering outside a locked competition venue. Today, we were *delighted* to see that in spite of arriving early enough to clean the plane and cook the onboard meal, our Air France flight was delayed. A couple of hours later they finally posted the gate and we scuttled off to check in, thankful that at least we could get rid of our baggage.

Before you all start oohing and aahing over the jet set life of a high-level athlete, let me tell you that Olympic qualification has its downsides: while competing, athletes are extremely short on cash because they are not able to work due to an insane travel schedule (case in point, six different countries in the first six weeks of the

2004 season). Thankfully, Olympic qualification also has its upsides. At the Olympics there are people at your beck and call, everything is free and you are treated like gold. However, the road there is rarely paved, and needless to say, we have gotten used to a certain low standard of living. As Canadian athletes, we make our own travel arrangements, book our own youth hostels, buy our own food to cook and always, *always* take public transportation. However, during the Olympic year when the Canadian Fencing Federation channels the budget toward the teams with the greatest chance of qualifying for the Olympics, things change a little.

When we arrived in Budapest, our coach Daniel walked directly to the taxi stand and we hesitated, tensing suspiciously like wary animals. Only when Daniel finally convinced us that he would pay for the taxi and get reimbursed by the Federation did we agree to get in. (Occasionally the Canadian Fencing Federation pays for all of our expenses, but not often. The coach's expenses are always covered by the Federation, so they tend to stay in hotels and take taxis, but coaches are generally pretty frugal too.) Once in the taxi, our driver struck up conversation in excellent English. He had recognized our bags as fencing equipment and told us how he used to be a pentathlete (five sports: fencing, pistol shooting, equestrian riding, running and swimming), and had competed in two Olympics. As Hungary was then part of the Eastern Block, he competed in Moscow in 1980 and then he was forced to boycott in 1984, but he competed in Seoul in 1988. I sat there nodding, my capitalist nature telling me that he was probably just trying to get a tip. When he mentioned some of the fencers he had competed against, I realized that he must have been telling the truth. Not only were they real fencers from a glorious time for the French team, but also Daniel Levavasseur, our coach, had coached them! Throughout the '80s they had won every title imaginable—from Olympic Champions to Hardest Partiers, I have been told. We laughed together as he told some of his own glory stories.

Since many former Olympians become coaches in their

"twilight years," I asked him why he became a taxi driver. He turned around, grinned at us and told us how taxi cab driving was like fencing: you see an opening and you just GO! Later, he explained that a lot has changed since the Communist era. Instead of coaching being a very prestigious and well-paid job, the few sessions of pentathlon training that he coaches every week only earns him $350 per month while driving a taxi brings in up to $2,000 per month.

Along with most of the other teams, we settled into the hotel, which was a nice change from our usual hostel bunk beds on the other side of town. The next morning we readied for the first Olympic team qualification of the year. We were ahead of the Americans in the point race for our zone so all we needed to do was protect the lead. We drew the Italians in the round of 16. Normally they are a tough team for us because they like to keep a close distance and parry a lot, while we prefer to be at a greater distance and have an "absence of blade"—little or no contact between our blade and that of our opponent—and tend toward single action when attacking. Our coach established a battle tactic that seemed so simple: let them come in and make the mistakes. Like most battles, not everything went according to plan, and we found ourselves down in the score after about four bouts. Luckily there are nine bouts in a team match (each fencer on a team of three must fence all three members of the other team, to a total of 45 points, or until time runs out), but even that didn't help us. I went in for the last bout with our team behind by four points. Facing me was Bianca Del Carretto. The last time I had fenced her was in 2003, when I had beaten her en route to winning the Modling World Cup in Austria. Hoping she would have flashbacks to that loss, I went after her like a starving bulldog after a bone. We needed this victory to stay ahead of the Americans! In a few minutes I had jumped ahead by three points, but unfortunately my brain then started working. A common mistake in a fencing match is the tendency to leave the "now" and start thinking of the future: the next round, the next opponent, what colour medal you may go home with ... This can really disrupt your focus and before you know it, "now" is over and there is no future for you—at least at that competition!

Knowing that I could move the team closer to an Olympic qualification by winning the match, I started thinking about marching in the Opening Ceremonies with my amazing team and lost track of the job at hand: winning the match! Suddenly, Del Carretto had tied the match 32–32, and there were only six seconds left. Suddenly my mind was clear: *I will not lose our opportunity to go to the Olympics!* Knowing that I had scored every time I attacked without letting her close the distance, I attacked—and scored!

With only two seconds left on the clock, we were now up by one hit and she didn't have time to catch me in those two seconds. As the buzzer rang to announce the end of time, I turned around and my four teammates and coach ran toward me laughing and cheering. I quickly dropped my épée and jumped up and down with them. Our only supporter, my good friend George, sauntered over and said in his thick Serbian accent, "Vell, team is getting somevhat exciting." The king of understatement.

The rest of the day was nowhere near as exciting because we all fenced sub-par, losing matches to Hungary, South Korea and the Ukraine, ending up in eighth position out of the 17 countries that participated. Thankfully, the USA was eleventh.

The individual event was two days later and I won my first two matches quite easily. My third match to go into the quarter-finals was against an Italian girl, Cristiana Cascioli, fighting tooth and nail to qualify herself individually for the Olympics. I couldn't keep up with her. When she beat me handily, running me ragged, I realized that I had to train harder. I am not the type of athlete who can let herself go and rely on pure, unbridled talent to win. Babe Ruth I'm not, although I think I *could've* competed with him in a hot dog eating contest! There is definitely some fencing talent in my genes but it has to be forced into the spotlight through lots and lots of hard work.

We spent the week in Budapest because the Prague World Cup

was just the next week, so this week became a training camp with two daily sessions of cardio or power training and fencing practice. The fencing training was excellent, if slightly unorthodox. The first night, we jumped in a cab and gave the driver a paper with the name and address of the fencing club. When the taxi stopped to let us out in front of a huge synagogue, I thought he was kidding. He insisted that this was correct so we heaved our fencing bags onto our shoulders and walked through the heavy wooden front doors, certain that we were going to interrupt some religious proceeding. Well what a surprise when we walked in to find a three-storey fencing club! Sabre was run on the first floor, foil on the second and épée on the top floor under beautifully domed mosaic ceilings decorated everywhere with the Star of David.

By Friday, our week of training in Budapest was over and I sadly left this city that has many of my favourite things: cheap, good opera, great cafés, mega-malls, comfortable movie theatres and my dear friend George. The only consolation is that we were going to Prague, which is beautiful, inexpensive, and the home of Good King Wenceslas.

Prague, Czech Republic.
January 31–February 1, 2004

I don't really understand why people would want to travel in Prague. Please don't assume that I am saying you should never go to Prague, because it is a beautiful city and well worth a visit. I am using the word travel in the strictest sense, as in, "to go from one place to another by some form of transportation." Every single form of transportation that I have experienced in Prague has been dodgy to say the least. My first time in Prague was in 1999, well after the fall of communism in Europe. However, corruption was still rampant and local crooks had an eye out for vulnerable travellers. The second day of competition was on a Sunday starting at eight in the morning. I was concerned that we might not arrive at the competition on time with public transit running infrequently, so I asked the hostel desk clerk to order me a taxi. An unmarked car pulled up right away. A scruffy looking driver with serious bed head sat impatiently tapping his hands on the steering wheel as he glared at the hostel door. Finally, he opened his car door and shouted, "Taxi?" followed by a string of muttered curses. Surprised that there seemed to be no sign indicating an official taxi car, and quite taken aback by his demeanour, I wasn't sure if I should get in, but time was running short and I had to get to the gym. I got in the car and in no more than five minutes we were there. I had no idea it was so close so I was pleased that the taxi would be cheap.

"Five hundred and ten koruny," he said.

"What!" It was the equivalent of 25 Canadian dollars. "That's impossible!"

"That's the price." He looked surlier than before and made no move to free my fencing bag from his trunk. "No meter and I can charge what I want."

"This is crazy, I am not paying that!"

"You have to or I get police," and he reached for his radio.

It was the oldest trick in the book, but I fell for it. "Okay, wait, I will go and get someone." I ran inside and grabbed hold of the president of the Czech Federation. Literally. He is over six-feet tall and *a lot* of man. "Help me!" I said, panting as I shook him. I explained the situation as best I could and he came out to help me confront this character. They negotiated back and forth with a lot of decisive, choppy hand talk that reminded me of how my Ukrainian grandmother would lecture us: "You have to lock all your car doors because strangers will jump in at red lights!" After a few minutes, my Czech friend came back to me and said, "Listen, I am sorry, he is a private taxi and he can pretty much charge whatever he wants so you really have to pay. I wish there was something I could do about it but unfortunately he can take advantage of you. Just be thankful that he didn't take you outside the city and leave you out in the woods somewhere." I couldn't believe my ears. Not only was I to pay this guy twice what I just paid for my hostel room, but now I was supposed to feel thankful that he didn't abandon me in the Czech countryside? This is getting around in Prague.

Wary after this experience, we rented a minibus taxi for everyone from the airport and established a price—either what was on the meter or a fixed price that seemed reasonable. The only mistake we made this time was putting Sophie Lamon (a Swiss fencer who happened to be travelling with us) and Monique, the two pretty blond girls, in the front to distract the driver. Like a sad, middle-aged man with a new sports car, he took off like a rocket, zipping around and changing lanes every few seconds— despite there being no one else on the road. As the roads became snowier, he drove faster. I honestly thought we were going to crash into the ditch. I imagined the headlines in the Canadian papers: "Choice to Attend World Cup Not Too Prague-matic." We were screaming at the driver, "SLOW DOWN! YOU ARE GOING TO KILL US! STOP THE VAN!" He didn't, and it was only by the grace of God we arrived at our hotel in one piece.

We were pretty jittery coming down from all the stress of the ride so we unpacked slowly and finally made our way down to the hotel restaurant. The day had been long and tense, and suddenly the English translation of the menu was funnier than usual. I have seen many a "Roast Sucking Pig," "Fried God Fish," and "Acidated Soda," but this was the first time I had seen a chef mixing table decor with cuisine. I ordered his proposed "Candlestick Beef" just to see what it might be. Would it be a chunk of meat shaped like a thick candlestick or sliced up to look more like a delicate cande-labrum? Well, my romantic notions of interesting cuisine were crushed as "Candlestick Beef" turned out to be a slice of roast beef bathed in gravy. Had it not been about the same price as a Starbucks latte, I would have been quite disappointed.

With a solid meat-and-potatoes supper in my belly, I was ready for the competition next morning. My first two matches were straightforward but then I came across a Norwegian girl, Margrete Moerch, who is very good at taking the blade. This essentially means that she could control my épée—either taking it while attacking, or taking it when I attacked—and secure a hit while making sure my blade was pointed anywhere but at her. I was ahead in the match, but near the end Margrete tied it up and won in overtime. So close to making the quarter-finals, and yet I still felt under-trained and so, so far from where I wanted to be as an athlete. I tucked that into my rapidly increasing bank of expe-rience and caught the first flight out of this city.

Saint Maur, France.
February 6–9, 2004

Finally, a weekend at home! After too much travelling, I was thankful that this World Cup was being held in the suburbs of my city of residence, Paris. I had plans to spend some quality time with my husband, sleep in my own bed and cook whatever I wanted for my pre-competition meal. The Canadian Fencing Federation had other plans.

This was another Olympic team qualification, so I was expected to stay at the hotel with the team. I woke up the day before the competition, packed my bag and took the city train to a suburb of Paris called Saint Maur. Then I checked myself in at the hotel and unpacked the bag I'd packed only an hour earlier and settled into my home not-away-from home. I must say, it was a nice change to turn on the TV and see more than a couple of goldfish! About a year before, Geordie had found an old television set and instead of repairing it, he gutted it and put our aquarium inside. It is much more relaxing than real television and there are no commercials, but as loving as they are when they chase each other after their daily feeding of green peas, Shane and Cindy will never have the Ross and Rachel connection, so I was delighted to watch a few brainless sitcoms.

Running With Swords

Before long it was time for dinner, something that had become quite a chore since acquiring a Frenchman to coach Team Canada. I have decided that it is a truly Canadian feature to enjoy variety. We love food from all over the world. If people ask me, "What is a typically Canadian meal?" I always have to say that it depends on your parents' heritage. For me, a typical Canadian meal is perogies and deer sausage, thanks to my Ukrainian maternal grandparents. For the Canadian girls on the team, a regular week of eating might include curry, fajitas, spaghetti, sushi and poutine, so we are ready for anything. For Daniel, a regular week would be steak, fries and salad, although if he was feeling a little crazy he might alternate pepper sauce with mustard atop his steak, the wild man.

Although he has travelled the world and will politely and gratefully eat anything put in front of him, Daniel insists that there are certain eating habits that must be maintained, *especially* before a competition. He dragged us to the same pub in Sydney, Australia, for *five straight nights* for their cheap steak and potatoes. "Don't change your habits!" is his big catchphrase for making us eat whatever he deems palatable for days on end. When he first became the Canadian national coach, we tried to make him understand Canadian cultural cuisine: "Coach, it *is* our habit to eat Chinese food. We cook it at least twice a week at home. Please don't make us eat more pizza!" Daniel is a truly despotic coach; there was no arguing or discussion. The only answer we ever received was, "Don't change your habits," as we walked into yet another pizza parlour. We always wondered if he would change his diet were he ever to coach the Chinese team ...

Saint Maur was no exception to this regimented diet but on the third night, the General had arranged a dinner with his friends, so we could finally have some food that didn't involve the word "Bolognese." We peered into the windows of a couple of different Chinese restaurants and eventually found the entire Chinese fencing team already seated and eating spring rolls. We took that as a sign that the food was good. If it was good enough for the girls from Beijing, it had to be good enough for the girls from Canada.

Sherraine MacKay

After our tasty meal we met back at the hotel for a team meeting where Daniel prepped us for the next day's event. Our first match would be very difficult. We were taking on the French team in France, with French media covering the competition.

They came out roaring, and we just weren't on our game and lost badly. To avoid getting too depressed, we cheered the Russians against the Americans and hoped they'd destroy them. To our surprise, the Americans were neck-and-neck with them right down to the last match. The entire Canadian team had a vested interest in Russia winning, because an American upset over the Russians could upset our chances at Olympic qualification. We watched in disbelief as the match went into overtime. You could have filmed it and sold it with the *Rocky* series for its drama and intensity. The Russian anchor for her team, Tatiana Logounova, is perhaps the coldest person on the circuit. I am sure that she is very nice in everyday Russian life, but she is an extreme example of an athlete "leaving their kindness at the door." I have seen match after match where her opponents come away humiliated because she has not only dominated the match but has laughed in their faces and imitated their last-ditch efforts to score some points. As if that weren't ignoble enough, she will also just stop trying and stand there with her arm extended like a statue, snickering and waiting for her opponents to lose their cool completely.

As offensive as she may be to the rest of the world, Tatiana is one of Geordie's best friends on the women's circuit, and there is one reason why. A few years ago, he inspired her to win her match. We were in Beijing, China, for the World University Games, and the team final was Russia against China. Being the host country, the Chinese had reserved 99 percent of the tickets for the loudest and most spirited home team spectators. Five thousand cheering people were led by the men's national coach, Jiao Dao. He had a big bass drum and a booming yell. While China was dominating the match, Jiao Dao was ruling the crowd, "*Jia yo*, China! *Jia yo*, China!" Literally translated this means, "Add some oil, China! Add some oil, China!" It was thunderous and unnerving. A far cry from the cheerful sing-song, "Let's go Ca-na-da, let's go," but I digress ...

Watching such a one-sided match was pretty boring for everyone but it especially irked Geordie, who complained, "I did not travel 15 hours on an airplane and then 25 hours on a train to see this walkover!" Our Canadian coach at the time, Guy Boulanger, leaned over to Geordie and tempted him, "You should do something about it!" After China had scored another point and with the crowd rocking the stadium roaring, "*Jia yo*, China!" Geordie stood up in the hush immediately following the din, clenched his fists, and with his monstrous lungs and rock-star vocal chords yelled, "JIA YO, RUSSIAAAAAAAAAAA!" All ten thousand eyes turned to settle on my husband, who was standing quivering and flushed after the release. Make that five thousand and two eyes; from her en guard position on the final piste, Tatiana Logounova turned and looked directly at Geordie. The fact that Tatiana took notice of him motivated Geordie even more, and for the rest of match he supported the Russians by answering every Chinese cheer with one for Russia with the same intensity (and maybe half the volume) of the crowd. When Tatiana scored a crucial point to bring her team close to equalizing, she let out a yell of victory and pointed her finger to the stands where I was cringing. Geordie was standing up next to me in his Canadian jersey, pointing right back at her. They had a connection that was eerie and I worried that if Russia actually ended up winning I would lose my husband to the local authorities. "Sit down, honey! Seriously, this is a communist country and victory is a matter of national pride. Who knows what they'll do to you, so SIT DOWN!"

Whether he heard me or not over the din, it appeared that Jiao Dao agreed with me, for he kept motioning Geordie to sit down with a condescending flapping of his hand. The Chinese crowd thought this motioning was a clapping pattern so they started in again and soon picked up momentum because China was again in a comfortable lead. No longer feeling cowed, Geordie started up again but his throat was going and during an especially soulful, "RUSSIAAAAAAAAA," his voice cracked. Almost everyone in the stands erupted into laughter at my 25-year-old husband, who had sounded like he had suddenly re-entered puberty. Feeling generous with certain victory on the horizon, Jiao Dao picked up his can of "Drinkable Happiness" (better known outside of China as Coca-Cola) and offered it to Geordie. As it had already been the happiness of Jiao Dao's mouth, Geordie politely declined and went back to cheering. The match was quickly over but not quickly forgotten. In between getting his photo taken with a bunch of Chinese children, Geordie was given hugs from the Russian silver medallists and Tatiana said, "How could I ever forget you?" They hadn't won the overall match but Geordie's support had inspired Tatiana to dominate her matches and I guess she felt eternally grateful.

Today at Saint Maur, a few more years into Geordie and Tatiana's relationship, I was for the first time completely behind her. For selfish reasons I wanted her to win so badly that I was holding my breath. The score: 44–44. The next point wins. The gym was completely silent. On the bench, the American girls were bouncing around nervously, and the Russians were chewing on their nails. The rest of the fencers in the gym were watching because nobody could believe it was this close. On the piste, the American hesitated and Tatiana did a flèche … and scored. I could breathe. Nobody moved for a few seconds as we were all watching how the two girls would react. The American took off her mask and solemnly held out her hand for the standard post-match hand-shake. Tatiana slipped her mask off, smirked at the crowd before briefly sliding her hand through the American's grasp, and headed outside for a nice, long, celebratory smoke. Russia had just served us up the U.S.

We were the next team to take on the Americans. We wanted to win not just to secure our Olympic berth but also to show that without question we deserved our place at the Olympics. We won the match by a large margin and didn't even need to join the Russians for a smoke afterwards …

Running With Swords

Later that night we did celebrate, but we did it Canadian style: sitting outside beside a river. In the overall rankings, we were ahead of the Americans by quite a few points and the Cubans hadn't even shown up for the competition, so the American zone looked to be ours for the taking! The reason that we were toasting our success on a riverbank instead of in a fancy restaurant is that in Europe, restaurants open at 7:30 p.m. at the earliest. So there we were at 6:15 standing in front of the closed, dark restaurant. Instead of walking back to the hotel, we decided to pick up something to drink at "Ed the Discount Grocer" and sit along the Marne to toast our nearly secure Olympic berth. After about an hour and a half we decided to go and eat but by now we were carrying empty bottles. Perhaps I should thank my father, relentless nature lover and Alberta's 1992 Conservationist of the Year, for my environmentally aware upbringing. Growing up, I actually had more fear of park rangers than I did of police. Police would only get you if you had broken a law, most of which you knew and if you were responsible, you made the choice not to break. Park rangers ruled their land KGB style with all sorts of obscure regulations. You were never sure if picking a flower or looking too closely at tree moss was going to land you in the clink.

I have carried my respect for the environment with me to France: a country composed of people who seem to think that garbage cans are modern art displays never to be touched. Through my behaviour I have become somewhat of an oddity. My father is admittedly maniacal about things like protecting National Park property, but an aversion to litter is bred into every Canadian. So, there we were after our riverside celebration, Canada's international sports representatives stomping into the restaurant with empty bottles as though we expected to pay for dinner with them. Walking into the restaurant we saw some members of the Swiss team primly sitting at a table drinking mineral water, eating salads and lean meat. Not wanting to flaunt the fact that we were probably qualified and they were not, we slipped our empty bottles to the barman and slunk into our chairs. The waitress first looked at us, then at the bottles and said, "What is this garbage?" As we started to explain that we just wanted to recycle our bottles rather than leave them by the river, we realized we should just shut up and order our meals. Fortunately, we can laugh at these kinds of things because that is what we'll remember when we are old, grey, and trying to entertain our grandchildren with stories from the good old days of Olympic fencing. While I probably will forget exactly how I won the Havana World Cup, I will never forget the look on that woman's face when we walked into her restaurant like a recycling parade.

My great-grandparents and the home in Poland that they left.

My grandpa Adolf and grandma Emilie and the whole family.
My young strapping dad is bottom right (in the overalls).

Age 8, in my sweet years before the swordplay. We always had a few pets to teach us "responsibility" and to catch the mice on the farm.

Dad, me, and Mom, after the 1993 Nationals.

Preparing for the World Champs in Cuba 2003. Above,
teammate Julie Leprohon making sure I am flexible.
At bottom, Daniel Levavasseur giving me a lesson.

Multi-tasking: stretching and thinking, which is harder than it looks
to be quite honest.

CAM

Pais | Nombre y Apellido

Comic relief in Cuba. I still don't remember what was so funny,
but I do know it wasn't Castro.

Doing what I love!

On the piste against Tatiana Logounova at the Athens Olympics,
to go to the gold medal match.
Thankfully, this photo shows one of my points!

Geordie and I in the CBC studio in Athens, with Brian Williams and Ron MacLean.

Inspired weirdness from the always crazy Canadian women's épée team. From left: me, Catherine Dunnette, Marie-Eve Pelletier, Monique Kavelaars, and Julie Leprohon.

My favourite part of fencing is tricking people,
and this expression shows it all.

Geordie and I in London at Picadilly Circus.
We were there for the Nickelback concert.

Tauberbischofsheim, Germany.
February 20–23, 2004

Preparations for the World Cup in Tauberbischofsheim, Germany, are more intense than for other competitions. Not just because it is one of the most competitive Grand Prix World Cups on the circuit, but because Tauberbischofsheim is a town dedicated almost entirely to fencing. Despite its meagre population of 10,000, it has the biggest fencing centre in the world, complete with permanent fencing pistes, an equipment shop, several gymnasiums, a swimming pool, dormitories, a cafeteria and best of all, saunas and tanning beds to achieve that, "I've just been vacationing in a small town in Germany" afterglow. If, however, at any point during your time spent in Tauberbischofsheim you do *not* want to be immersed in the glorious sport of fencing, you'll have a hard time finding anything else to do. Of course, there is the standard café and church tour found in most European villages, but beyond that there are only restaurants that serve up steaming portions of pork knuckles and litres of beer. Not exactly the ideal pre-competition activity for our final Olympic qualification trial.

I had always thought it was the sheer grandeur of this fencing centre that made officials put reflective road signs—with a little stickman fencer—showing how to get to Tauber from the highway, but I have come to realize instead that Germans just love to put up bizarre road signs. On the outskirts of Tauber there are big triangular signs in red warning the passing traffic of, bizarrely enough, "Toad Crossing," the weirdest and cutest sign I can remember.

On the road into town, we passed rolling green hills and four-lane highways. Suddenly the wind changed. The skies turned dark and chunks of snow started whipping into our windshield. We saw Daniel grip the steering wheel a little tighter and sit up a little straighter. Tension threatened to pervade the atmosphere of the minibus until Julie Leprohon chirped, "Whooo hoo! It's like Canada!" Julie, along with Marie-Eve and Catherine have been training and competing in Europe for five straight weeks now, and I realized then how much they really must have missed Canada to get nostalgic over a snowstorm! We all laughed, and when Daniel finally dropped us off at the youth hostel in Tauberbischofsheim we congratulated him for becoming a little more Canadian.

When we arrived at the youth hostel, Monique, Julie, Marie-Eve, Catherine and I settled in—girl style. We always laugh at how different we are from the guys' team. They would walk in, throw their bags on the floor and go out for a drink somewhere in town. When we walk into a hostel, we pay, organize the receipts, carry our luggage to our room, choose beds, put the sheets on our beds, unpack our bags and hang our giant Canada flag on the curtain rod. Then, when all of these steps are completed, we go to the grocery store to pick up supplies for the next day of fencing.

The next day, Daniel had scheduled a light training session for the afternoon when we were supposed to take one-on-one lessons. While the coach always wears the thick leather jacket and mask because he is the one getting hit all the time, the level of security for the athlete varies according to country. In Paris, the athlete is required to wear a mask and a glove, but they are free to wear shorts and a T-shirt and not the full fencing uniform. In Brazil, it is the same deal with the mask and glove, but because of the heat and their, shall we say, "eye-catching" style of dress, you can pretty much take a lesson in your bikini. China, unsurprisingly, is the most incomprehensible of all. While its athletes actually take high-speed lessons *without* masks, Chinese athletes frowned upon our choice of shorts for training because they exposed too much of our bodies. Here in Germany I was disappointed to see that all the athletes were taking lessons in full fencing uniforms. A full fencing uniform—chest protector, jacket, pants, long socks, glove, and a mask—can be stuffy and is a pure bother to put on simply for a lesson. Hoping that I could get out of it, I motioned to one of the directors of the centre and, when he came over, I asked him if I *absolutely must* wear a full uniform to take a lesson. It was Matthias Behr, a famous fencer, Olympic Medallist, and World Champion during the '80s. When I pleaded with him to let me wear only shorts and a T-shirt, he looked disgusted and said, "Please, I am telling you … it is for your own safety!" Suddenly, it dawned on me that I was asking permission to fence without proper protection from a man who had accidentally killed someone with his foil in the heat of the 1982 World Championship semi-final. Granted, the equipment was nowhere near as secure as it is now, but when his broken foil pierced the mask of his Russian opponent, Vladimir Smirnov, I am sure he found no consolation in knowing that the accident was entirely due to faulty equipment. After Smirnov's death, the International Fencing Federation raised its safety standards, and all fencers are now required to put their masks through a safety check before each competition. If a mask is deemed too old or damaged, the fencer cannot compete unless he or she can find a new mask. No wonder that everyone in the training centre was fully covered and protected with Matthias Behr in charge.

The next day in the team competition the French were ferocious, hitting us 45 times to our 39 and winning the match. There was no beating around the bush for them; they had to finish first overall at this World Cup, which was their last hope to earn an Olympic berth. Considering that the French team had the strongest individuals in the world and that the other countries that had already secured their positions for the Olympics had sent their junior teams, there wasn't much stopping them. Germany had its senior team present but one couldn't help but notice that their concentration was perhaps on the celebration of "Carnival" when they showed up with red clown noses and striped socks to fence in the final.

Gaining an Olympic berth depended on one thing: the Americans had to finish lower than third at this competition. This would guarantee that our world ranking would be higher, and we could take the American zone. Considering that they had not yet made a top eight result in any World Cup in the past few years, their chances were slim, but fencing can be unpredictable. After our match with France I noticed my coach intently watching the piste where the Americans were fencing China, hoping to enter the top eight. Up until their ninth and last bout, China was winning handily. Then the Americans made a brave comeback and were within a few points of victory when time ran out. With the chance for an American medal no longer a possibility, we were guaranteed a spot at the Olympics! I turned to my teammates and as we shook each other's hands, smiling and congratulating ourselves for a berth well earned, I think I saw Daniel get a few years younger.

The rest of the team competition went well enough as we ended up finishing 11th (losing to France and the Ukraine but beating Greece and Italy). As disappointed as I was to lose to the Ukraine, I took advantage of their post-victory benevolence to trade a track jacket with them. My mother is of Ukrainian heritage and she would love prancing around in East European style!

We toasted our qualification with our traditional celebration drink: a mix of lemonade and beer. Sitting on the floor in front of our bunk beds we munched on pretzels, laughing and talking about everything *except* the obvious change in our goals. Now the battle had shifted from "Team Canada versus the rest of the world" to a sort of civil war, where everyone besides me had to fight it out to see who would take the remaining two individual positions on the Canadian Olympic team. My place was secure, as I was ranked number one in Canada. Catherine, Monique, Julie and Marie-Eve would have to battle it out for the remaining spots. With any other team this could have turned very ugly, very fast, but these women are extraordinary. While they will fight tooth and nail to earn their position, they will also respect and encourage each other, knowing that we have all worked as a cohesive unit of five to qualify the team of three that will compete at the Games.

The individual competition was, as usual, held over two days and only three of us qualified for the second day elimination round. Unfortunately, Monique and Catherine lost their first matches. Fortunately, I won my first one against an Italian girl. My second match was against a Russian who kept it really even, and before I knew it, we were tied 14–14. Since she was quite aggressive, I hesitated on how to approach the last point. Should I attack to shut down her attack, or should I let her come and hit her on the way in … Well, I didn't have much time to make my choice because she came blasting in. I reacted by ducking low so her point flew above my head, and I hit her on the chest as she lunged forward. Success! I moved into the round of 16 where I met up, once again, with my nemesis!

For the past 11 years, Imke Duplitzer and I have been fencing on the same circuit. I don't expect her to remember, though, as I was just one more of her victims once upon a time. Imke has had a stellar career, remaining in the Top 16 in the world for several years. I took her in the final of the Sydney World Cup and led her the whole match. She tied it up at the end and we fenced off for the last point. When I landed the last hit for the championship I felt like I'd won the Olympics.

At the World Cup in Tauberbischofsheim, we met up once again. In a rare moment of inconsistency, Imke had fallen out of the Top 16 ranking and was obliged to fence in the first day of eliminations. She had fenced well and we now met on the second day. Fencing is a sport of concentration and explosion, and the explosion often manifests itself after the point is won in an energy-charged victory yell. (Apparently there was a study done at the

Atlanta Olympics of the sport with the loudest screams per decibel and men's weightlifting was loudest with women's épée a very close second.) In an all-too-common moment of obvious, in-your-face aggression, Imke reared back and let out a blood-curdling scream, this time before the match began. In my shock I mused, either this is a new motivation technique, a psyche-out play, or this girl needs some therapy. The match started off well enough, and we were close until the last three minutes, but I just didn't have the stamina to keep up with her. Maybe I should have tried yelling … it's all the rage in Tauber.

Thankfully, as intense as they are about training, Germans are equally intense about partying. Every year after the final they roll out the barrel and the sober athletic factory turns into a beer garden where lederhosen-wearing waitresses serve up bratwurst and pretzels all to the tune of a live brass band. Maybe that is why, of all the World Cups, the village of Tauberbischofsheim has by far the most spectators—with nearly five thousand people! If there was unlimited Chianti at the Legnano World Cup and they handed out, say, personal bank accounts at the Zurich World Cup, I am sure spectator attendance would be higher there as well.

Sion, Switzerland.
February 23–30, 2004

Every year, Daniel arranges a "training camp" with his very good friends the Lamon family, who live and train in Sion, Switzerland. I don't know what kind of operation the Swiss are running but I think it should be called a "fattening camp." One would think that the program of skiing all day and fencing all night would whip us into shape. What we didn't know is that every day begins at 10:00 with thick slices of bread, pastries and hot chocolate. The skiing part of the program starts after our food is digested and, when we weren't coasting down glacial mountains we were being chairlifted up. On our "rest day" we went tobogganing. When I was young, tobogganing involved a lot of work because you had to stomp your Sorel boots up a snowy hill for at least 15 minutes and then sit on a red plastic saucer flying down the hill for a mere 15 seconds. Like clocks and chocolate, the Swiss have perfected tobogganing and it is now an art form. Basically, you avoid any physical exertion as the chairlift takes you up to the same exit as the skiers. You put your butt on a wooden sled and just coast down the hill for a few kilometres, stopping only for coffee breaks and deer crossing.

I must backtrack a bit where I referred to skiing as "coasting down glacial mountains." To be honest, there is never any "coasting" when I have skis strapped to my feet. There is hyperventilating, trembling and falling, but never any coasting. Daniel prides himself on his psychological preparation of his athletes and, when he heard that I was afraid to ski, he knew this was his chance to push my limits and make me face my fears. Of course someone else's fears are always irrational, and mine were completely unfounded to Daniel. We were going skiing in the Swiss Alps and my first ever run would be on a glacier called "Dead Plain." Out loud I said, "Yeah, let's go, Coach," but inside I was reliving my experiences from my last ski trip. The pain, the tears, the disbelief—and the pain.

I was eight years old. For the first six years of my life my parents had taken us on yearly ski trips, and I was actually quite capable. I remember zooming straight down the Bunny Hill as a four-year-old, doing jumps at the end of the hill. When I was seven, we didn't go skiing for some reason so the next time I hit the slopes, I was already eight and had undergone quite a growth spurt. Jonene and I were skiing together on the "Deer Run," which was not very difficult if you can do more than point your skis straight down the hill and let 'er rip. I couldn't do much more than that and in the midst of trying I plowed straight into a snow bank and landed with a crunch on my right foot. In about five seconds, when the shock had worn off, I started wailing with pain. Jonene snowplowed over to where I lay a puddle of tears.

"Get up, you're embarrassing me," she hissed with early adolescent pride. "I mean it! If you don't get up now, I am leaving!" I looked up at her to beg her not to leave but I couldn't find the space to talk in between my tears. With such a scene on the hill, the ski patrol soon arrived in their Red Cross jackets, holding a stretcher.

"Can we help you girls out?" they asked.

"No," Jonene said, smiling sweetly, "my sister is okay. Really. She just fell, but it happens all the time. She's fine."

Running With Swords

"Uh, I guess if she's really all right, yeah we could go check the rest of the hill ... Good luck and be careful girls!"

I sat there and watched as my only hope of salvation swooshed away.

"Great ... now what am I supposed to do? Why did you send them away?" I gasped in between sobs.

"Oh, stop being such a baby and ski down the hill." Nowadays, motherhood has changed Jonene into a soft-hearted, excellent wife and mother of two wonderful sons, but at that time she could be a real taskmaster. Just as I had started to cry again out of pain and despair, an angel in a navy blue coat and a red beard came skiing up to us and offered to help me down the hill to the lodge.

When I was back at the lodge, my parents came to see what was wrong. My dad took a look at my leg and didn't see any broken bone sticking out so he assessed it as a sprained ankle. A second opinion was definitely in order, but because we were on the first day of our week-long, yearly ski vacation my health was put on hold. "Since it's only a sprained ankle, we'll wait to see the doctor once we get back to Brooks," was my dad's decision. I was thankful when the week of hobbling around the hotel looking like a crab and being carried into restaurants drew to a close. We finally drove home and the next morning was church. As we were parking the car, my dad turned to my mom: "I think I am going to take Sherraine to the emergency room. She is still complaining about that ankle. We'll see you in a bit."

A few hours later we showed up, catching the tail end of the church potluck dinner. I walked in on one leg and two crutches. Sprained ankle, indeed! I had a fractured tibia and now wore a cast from my toes to my hip.

With that memory in my mind, I was on my way up the Swiss Alps in a chairlift. The first advice I was given from one of the experienced skiers was to go slowly. As if I could make that choice. All I knew how to do was tuck my poles under my arms, point my skis down the hill and let 'er rip. The second piece of advice I received was, "If you find yourself going too fast, just turn and ski back up the hill, letting gravity stop you." So while every other skier and snowboarder was carving snake-like patterns down the hill, I was making huge, lopsided smiles on the face of the mountain. At one point I was going with such speed that I couldn't turn. I really tried, but I just cut a straight line across the hill, barely crossing the trail without getting slammed into by another skier as I headed for the edge of the run. Well, as I speeded toward it, I had no idea it was a ditch until I went flying up a little incline and came crashing down the other side. Daniel, Monique and some of my other teammates had stopped when they heard my kamikaze yell. They were standing and watching as I arose from the white nothingness, first, toque askew with my two braids poking out, wearing one ski and a face full of rage. "I HATE THIS SPORT!" I yelled as I plunged my poles—which I had somehow managed to retain during all the chaos—into the snow. "Calm yourself," said Daniel. Monique knew better than to try to calm me down and went off to find my other ski. The remainder of the ski trip was as disastrous as its beginning, but by the end I did manage to control my emotions a bit better—mostly by considering this some sort of penance—so maybe Daniel had achieved his end in a weird way.

After spending all of that morning eating, skiing during the day and fencing in the evening, we were ready to head back to Paris for some normal training. Our next World Cup was in about a month so we could pack away our passports and travel toothbrushes for at least a few weeks.

Budapest, Hungary.
April 18–24, 2004

P art of being an amateur athlete means cutting costs. While Paris has been unquestionably positive for my sports career, it has, surprisingly enough, given me no edge in the beauty department. It's just too expensive to be beautiful in Paris. In Canada, my esthetician, Vivene, would wax all my unmentionables for a truly amateur-athlete price. Here in Paris, they are less sympathetic, because this is the city of beauty and people will pay their exorbitant fees. My solution: warm paraffin self-torture.

There are many major self-discoveries that take place in the darkest moments of one's life. If you ever want to understand your own personal approach to dealing with pain, just pour some hot wax on your armpit and observe the psychological process you undergo in order to rip it off. My teammate Monique grits her teeth and does a countdown to prepare for the excruciating pain of "the rip." After many rips of my own, I have come to understand how I deal with things that I hate but have to do: don't think about it too much. For instance, if I tell myself that I will rip on the count of three, I will count out loud, "one, two, three ... four, five, six," and think "oh, what the heck, I may as well go to ten." At which point

I count to every next series of ten until the wax is too hard and must be chipped off with a metal spatula, leaving me in bona fide agony. So now I realize that I am not a countdown girl; I need to just go for it before I start to over-think.

This holds true for my approach to training. If it is something that I don't really like to do, like long runs or long footwork sessions, I don't do the countdown, I just start the instant I get my shoes on. The longer I postpone it, the more distasteful it becomes. I could say, "Oh I'll go running later," but by then it's become rush hour and the streets are packed with Parisians storming home after work. And let's face it, Parisians are about as willing to step aside on the street as they are to pick up dog poo. But if I postpone my run until after rush hour, night has fallen and I will face relentless solicitations: "Hey, mademoiselle, you want a coffee with me?—Marry me?—You are beautiful ... what? You don't even answer? ... You think you are too good for me? ... You are nothing, nobody! ... I hate you."

Thanks to this self-discovery in a tin of wax, I know that for highly stressful situations, say skiing on a Swiss glacier or attending the Olympic Games or setting out for a training camp, I cannot spend time doing a countdown and preparing myself for the pain. I just have to bite down on a stick to stop the screaming and get to business.

With a "long" break of three-and-a-half weeks in between competitions, Daniel wanted to whip us back into shape. He arranged for us to participate in a training camp in Tata, Hungary, a small town about an hour outside of Budapest. They had built the training facility for the Hungarian's preparation for the 1948 London Olympics, and since they had a record number of medals there, the training centre has been kept in impeccable condition. The Hungarians were going to be training at this site and Daniel knew that with such strong opponents, it would be great sparring. As

Running With Swords

athletes training under Daniel for the past three years we knew to be ready for anything and had no hopes, either good or bad, because they were sure to be dashed.

Predicting the level of difficulty of a training camp is impossible to do, even if it's your coach organizing it. When we went for a training camp in Brazil two years before in December 2002, I went with expectations of ... well ... Brazil. I envisioned our cardio training as leisurely jogs on the boardwalk of Copacabana beach and daily sunbathing. Probably our coordination exercises would be learning how to samba. I don't remember ever being more wrong.

The camp took place in a military fort located on a stunning beachside in Rio de Janeiro, which shows the paradox we lived for the next two weeks. We slept in hard bunks with no air conditioning in 45-degree weather but ate at a fantastic restaurant every morning, noon and night. We were woken up at the crack of dawn military style but spent all day doing a sport that we love! We had orders barked at us non-stop but these orders came from our trusted coach ... or so we thought! Daniel, who was until that point a normal, friendly, charismatic man, turned into Attila the Hun. Our mornings were early, the cardio was impossibly hard, fencing sessions were long and we were *never, ever* good enough.

We did a VO2 max test, which is painful at the best of times. Basically, you have to sprint around a track at top speed and see how much oxygen your lungs can hold at the end of each lap. By the 10th lap or so, you want to scream in agony, but I'm sorry, you can't, because there is no oxygen left in your lungs. To really test our limits, Daniel decided to schedule the test at 12:00 noon. So, after our morning fencing session, just when the sun was at its highest and hottest, there we were running around a rubber track. Just beside us was the famous "Sugarloaf" mountain that normally provides a good amount of shade. At noon hour all it did was block any hope of a breeze. To make it even more painful, we could hear the ocean waves rolling onto the beach a few metres beyond our reach as we staggered around the track to the sound of Daniel screaming, "Relax your shoulders, go faster, take longer strides ... *go faster*!"

It was not all pain and torture. This was Rio de Janeiro after all! There was always so much beauty to see. All you had to do was lift up your fatigued head to see some of it. One evening I was plodding back to the dorms after a weight training session. It had been pouring rain most of the afternoon, but on my return the sun poked out before setting. I was walking along the length of the beach when I noticed two fishermen just standing there, looking up to the sky. My gaze followed theirs and I saw a double rainbow stretching from horizon to horizon across the ocean! When one experiences real beauty, a natural instinct is to share it with somebody, and while we were all in awe standing there, one of the fishermen walked over to me and said in Portuguese, "E bonita, no?" Of course, I agreed that it was beautiful. As we were nodding in disbelief at what was taking place before us, they said, "Deus e incroiabel!" I agreed that God was amazing, and we stood there admiring nature showing off some of her best for two old fishermen and a sweaty athlete.

Late in the week, when our energy levels had reached rock bottom and there was still a sprint session scheduled in that day's training, Daniel had a brainwave: he would motivate us by having us run on the beach! Nice idea, if you have the extra oomph to run on a soft surface and if you don't mind sand in your shoes and stares of incredulity from sunbathers. We went out on the beach and he marked the finish line, sent us back 50 metres and told us to sit down cross-legged with our backs to him. On his command we were to jump up, turn around and sprint to the end. This demands many levels of concentration; you have to stand up without wrenching your back, turn around without spraining your ankle and most important, win. So there we were, lined up like the characters from *Chariots of Fire*. Monique, who is an excellent sprinter, was certain to be one of the winners, and she was smart enough to choose to sprint on the harder, wet sand close to the water, which gave her an even greater advantage. What she didn't know, however, was that The Almighty was on my side that day. Just as Daniel shouted "GO!," a wave came crashing up onto shore where Monique sat oblivious to everything besides the race, and she was hit with 50 gallons of seawater! That gave me a huge head start, and for the first and only time in our athletic careers, I finished ahead of her in a foot race.

We grinned and bore the pain for the whole 10 days and then we were ready for the much needed Christmas vacation. For a total shock to my system, I flew directly from summertime in Rio to a snowstorm on the Albertan prairies. With the wind chill too extreme to do any sort of outdoor activity, I took this as a time to indulge in Mom's cooking, visits from old friends and a much-required mental recovery from the madness of the training camp. During my eggnog-induced reflection I realized why our coach had been so demanding in Brazil. In a training camp in China a few weeks prior to Brazil, Daniel had not worked us hard enough. He felt ashamed that after threatening us with the horrors of Chinese training, we didn't even break a sweat at the actual camp. In the weeks before we flew off to the land of rice for breakfast, rice for lunch and why not rice for supper, Daniel had filled our heads with stories about the camp he ran in China in 1989. He spoke of 14-hour days, inedible food and how he accidentally pierced a student but she continued to take her lesson in spite of the bleeding from her chest cavity. "Oh, you girls are going to come home knowing what *real* training is like! I lost 25 pounds in 2 weeks!"

When the time came and Monique and I stepped off the airplane, we were honestly petrified. We imagined armed guards waiting for us at the airport. Contrary to our nightmares, we were met at the Beijing International Airport by a lovely, gentle and very discreet man who stood no higher than my nose. Daniel introduced this man as Monsieur Wu, our host and translator. We called him Mr. Wu for the first few days until he left us a note and signed it Mr. Hu! With his French accent, Daniel couldn't say the letter *h* properly, but Mr. Hu refused to correct us because we were his guests.

We grew to like Mr. Hu a lot; not only was he our translator, he was our only friend. You see, the Chinese girls were a little more closed than most athletes from other countries, and it had nothing to do with their comprehension of English. I have spoken to several of them since and they understand English quite well. In fact when they came to train at the Racing Club in Paris, they understood my English as quickly as their translator did. Daniel had warned us about training in countries that don't have a regular turnover of foreigners. They would not want to spar very much, and when they did, chances are they would hide their true style. I guess they fear losing the element of surprise if they show their real chops. While I know that is a common approach (training in secret, not showing your real moves in practice, et cetera), I refuse to be a part of it. The fact remains that when you're good, you're good, and there is nothing your opponent can do about it. Even if everyone in the world knows that I am going to fake to the hand and drop to the foot, they will all fall for it if I set it up and execute it well.

At the start of the camp, Daniel told us to play by the same tactics and pick a false move to throw in once or twice during our matches. Being a novice at this, I picked something pretty basic and, I thought, pretty dumb. The trouble with this move was that it worked! Every time I tried it, I scored. I wondered if they were sharking me, and soon I was dizzy with second-guessing myself.

The general approach to training was completely different in China. Instead of doing one longer session like we do in Paris, they trained two or three times per day but for short periods. Overall it is probably better for your body but three showers per day became a little much for me. The first day was a real learning experience. Monique and I came ready to fence but they told us not to come to training because we were too tired after the trip. So we stayed in our freezing cold room, under the covers wearing sweatpants, sweatshirts, toques and socks, watching CNN until suppertime. After supper, we expected to train, so we milled around with the Chinese girls outside of their dorms.

Running With Swords

When they saw their coach arrive, the girls rushed outside in the freezing cold wind. Moe and I followed. Their coach, a soft-spoken man, quietly said a few words in Chinese. Instantly the girls assumed their positions in a line that seemed to be organized according to the coach's most preferred to his least preferred. Sensing this, Monique and I slipped to the back of the line. We exchanged quick looks thinking, "This is it, army training has begun!" We jogged off as a group to the gymnasium. Once we were inside, safe from the bitter cold, we started our warm-up. We jogged around the gym keeping careful watch to do exactly as the girls did, because we understood nothing that was said. After only two laps they all stopped and formed a huge circle. The male fencers were doing the same warm-up, and when the girls formed the circle, each of the guys went and paired up with a girl. Hoping this was not some sort of Chinese dating game, I paired up with Monique. The coach tapped one couple and blew his whistle, and we began a game of tag: my nightmare. More running for Sherraine.

Our training continued at the same leisurely pace. The most taxing thing was not the footwork or the daily runs but the social obligation that came with being Daniel's students. The Chinese Federation was so pleased that he had come to do the coaching clinic that they wanted to show him and his two girls a wonderful time. How do you spell "wonderful" in Chinese? K-A-R-A-O-K-E. Of the nine nights we were in China, six of them were spent in karaoke bars. When Monique and I weren't singing, we were expected to dance because we were often the only two women at these functions. Sing, dance, sing, dance. It was quite a training camp! Our hosts' favourite request was that we sing the *Titanic* theme song, which we dutifully performed. By the end of the week, the lyrics had changed from "My heart will go on" to "This camp can't go on." But it did.

In a final analysis of the Brazil and China camps, we decided that we much preferred to be completely exhausted from training than from singing and dancing. Knowing all the lyrics to

"Heartbreak Hotel" is not going to help you when it is 14–14 at the Olympics.

As we made our way to Tata to train with the Hungarians we had really no idea of what to expect. Would it be too easy? Too hard? Would we be forced to go out and party every night or run sprints in the beating sun? There was just no knowing. Well, like Goldilocks, we finally found one that was "just right."

The accommodations were fantastic. Modern double rooms complete with showers, drying racks for all our sweaty clothes, MTV and Eurosport! The compound was gorgeous with dark wood trim on all the buildings and lush flower gardens. There were excellent facilities: gyms, weight rooms, track, pool, hot tub and sauna, and the best part, a path around an adjacent lake where every morning we did a short run.

How you define "short" can be quite subjective. For some, it is less than two blocks; for others, it can be 45 minutes. Sometime around 7:00 a.m. we were all supposed to get up and do a lap around the lake. The second morning, Moe and I got up and went down to the lake where we met up with Krisztian Kulcsar, a member of the Hungarian National Men's Épée team. He is a giant. His face is very gentle and he is quite lean, so if you happen to be sitting down talking with him it is always surprising when he stands up. He just keeps going up, up, up and you wonder how anyone ever gets close enough to him to score a point.

Krisztian was just getting ready to start his morning run so Monique and I joined him. Jogging with him was like asking a class of preschoolers to keep pace with Shaquille O'Neal. The sound of our jog had a pound, patter-patter-patter, pound, patter-patter-patter as we took three little steps to equal one of his. Trying to chat while putting in such an effort is even more difficult! He and Monique talked away but I was focusing on the finish line thinking, "Man, will I be happy when this lap is over!" As we came back to

Running With Swords

our starting place, I saw both Krisztian and Monique hesitate. I hoped they were not going to keep running … this pace was too fast for me already, and I didn't know if I had it in me to do another lap like that. I wasn't one to make waves, though, so I said to myself, "If they keep running, then I guess I have to as well!"

Krisztian glanced at Monique, whose running is her glory, and she glanced at me but I was too busy trying to keep up to notice she was silently asking me, just as Krisztian had with Monique, "May we stop now without losing face?" The finish line came and went and the race continued. By the time we finished, it was almost time for breakfast but I was so exhausted I could barely walk back to the dorms. "Well, see you at breakfast!" Krisztian said cheerfully, and Monique waved back with equal enthusiasm. Her big grin was pasted on her face until she and I walked into our room and we immediately collapsed on our beds in a heap.

"What are you doing running that fast?" I scolded when I could finally muster the energy. For me that was like a 20-minute sprint! I could barely keep up, and we still have the whole day of training ahead of us!"

"Sorry, but Krisztian seemed to want to keep running after we had finished the first lap and he keeps a pretty good pace with his height. Let's try to run alone tomorrow, okay?"

Later that day I cornered Krisztian. I have no pride when it comes to running so I didn't mind asking him why he gunned it for two laps! "I didn't want to do two laps but your friend Monique looked like she wanted to keep on going after the first lap, and she set the pace pretty fast … I've been wiped out all day!"

This says something about high-level athletics: even with your friends—sometimes especially with your friends—nobody's instincts will let them back down.

Later in my lesson, Daniel reprimanded me for being so slow and tired. "What is your problem … are you totally out of shape after three weeks with no competitions?"

"No, coach, it is because of all the competition this morning." I explained the situation, and after calling me stupid for wasting my energy, we returned to business. First I am out of shape, and then I'm too keen. With coaches there is always something wrong and seldom any praise. What can you do?

This training camp was well balanced because while each session was intense, it was short and followed with a hot tub or sauna! At least it was supposed to be a hot tub. After our first day we were told to put on our swimsuits and come to the pool. Monique had not brought her suit because we rarely, if ever, go swimming at training camps, especially in a landlocked country like Hungary. Catherine and Julie had brought theirs because they had packed for a six-week stay in Europe to culminate in a World Cup on a coastal Spanish town of Marbella, where the only consolation in losing early is that you get to spend longer on the beach. Honestly, I had no idea we'd be swimming either, but since I had just bought a new bathing suit I wanted to bring it. Had I bought a new pair of mukluks or a new cocktail dress I would have found some luggage space for them as well.

So we showed up at the pool and most of the people were already in. We quickly slipped into our bikinis and walked out onto the deck … where every Hungarian athlete was wearing a streamlined racing suit and goggles. There were the three giggling Canadians in their floral print two-pieces getting goose pimples from the cold air. We felt like we'd crashed a formal cocktail party in jeans and tank tops. We spied a hot tub, and since Daniel had told us this was to be a short relaxation session we thought, what better way to relax than to bob around in the hot tub? I was the first to get in and once again pride made the decision for me. The tub had been started a few minutes earlier and the water had not been given the chance to warm up, so it was cold. Not cool, cold. We three sort of sat half-in, half-out of the tub until some Hungarians came over and dipped their feet in. "Oh! It's cold!" they said as they walked away. Now we looked even weirder for sitting in a cold tub so we just called it quits and went back to the change room where we stepped out of our delicates and back into our track pants where we belonged. After the tub warmed up, the rest of the training camp was a real treat.

Perhaps another reason why it was such a great camp was because we were able to watch hockey. The NHL playoffs were on and we all had a vested interest. Julie, who comes from Laval, Quebec, was always on the internet checking up on how her Montreal Canadiens were doing. Monique is a Leafs fan. I became a Senators fan by default when I married one of their biggest supporters. Catherine, who is from Calgary, was the most intense of all, and rightfully so because the Flames went to the finals that year. She would get e-mails from her sisters telling her of how many people around Calgary were wearing red wigs and tying Flames flags to their car antennas. We would all read up on our teams and catch glimpses of the highlights on Eurosport. With all that teasing, what we really wanted was to see a whole game. Our wish was granted but not in the way we expected.

My brother-in-law, Jeff Shantz, who plays in Switzerland, had qualified for Team Canada that year. To prepare for the World Championships in Prague, they came to Budapest to play an exhibition game. It happened to coincide with our Tata training camp. Jeff sent me an e-mail saying that he was there and if we wanted to come and watch the game he could get us all free tickets. We were dying to go! Of course we had to ask Daniel's permission: he would have the final word on it, as all activities, extracurricular as well, affect the success of a training camp. He denied permission because it was too last-minute and too complicated to arrange, but I have a feeling his refusal ran deeper than that. His dislike for the game of hockey dated back to our training camp in Montreal two years earlier.

The Canadian officials wanted to take Daniel out to a Canadian cultural event; and what better than to watch an arena of screaming fans cheer a bunch of guys as they bumped, punched and swore at each other. I know, I know, hockey is more than that, as my husband would be the first to tell me. So part of Daniel's experience in Canada was to go to a hockey game, drink some draft beer and eat a greasy hotdog. The game was back and forth and it was pretty exciting. Halfway through, the crowd was chanting "GO HABS GO!" Daniel loved this fervour; I guess it reminded him of European soccer matches. He turned to me excitedly and asked, "What are they saying?" Remember, his English is limited to the words, "rocker man" and "I speak very well English."

"Oh, it's just a local cheer." I tried to downplay it, knowing that it would pique his interest even more.

"What is it? I want to know!"

"Okay, repeat after me: Go eat shit" I said blandly.

He repeated it slowly and I corrected some minor mispronunciations to make sure he was saying it clearly. The French tend to pronounce their *i* like "ee" so it sounds as if he was telling someone to go eat some bedding. Saying it several times slowly, he gained enough confidence to say it louder, and in a few seconds was yelling it out at the crowd and punching the air with his fist on each syllable. I was almost crying I was laughing so hard and every time he looked back at me for encouragement, I thought my stomach muscles were going to tear. At the height of his crescendo, Julie's head whipped around. She was sitting a row away and had finally understood what Daniel was shouting. "What are you doing?" she asked, shocked.

"Sherraine told me the chant, so I am supporting your team."

Then Julie explained to Daniel what he had been yelling at the top of his lungs. When he turned to face me, he gave me a look of total betrayal. I laughed even more because, given the opportunity, he would have done exactly the same thing to me!

Thus, when it came to attending my brother-in-law's game, this time in Budapest, Daniel was not very enthusiastic and he found a way to say no. We ended up staying in our rooms and watching it on TV. We hung up our Canadian flag and sat around cheering Jeff and the gang. As nice as it is to have my brother-in-law play a professional sport, I am never sure whether it has been good or bad for my career. Of course, there are perks: with his substantially larger income he has been one of my regular sponsors. Training for a living also gives him an insight on how to deal with anything from negative feedback to slumps. The downside to being so close to a pro athlete is that I have seen the complete inequality of funding between amateur and professional sports first-hand. It has nothing to do with the amount of training or expertise of either athlete; a high-performance amateur and a professional put in similarly long hours to become the very best. It has everything to do with the surrounding support group, treatment both on the road and at home and, most crushingly, the paycheque at the end of the day.

This was on my mind quite a bit late one night just after the Tata camp as I was tossing and turning and unable to sleep, not because the beds were lumpy or the neighbours were noisy, but because I was inhaling the pungent smell of a sweaty gymnasium because that's where I was sleeping! When my brother-in-law was with the hockey team, they enjoyed four-star luxury of the Sofitel across town. I remember seeing his itinerary when he was in Budapest. It went something like: breakfast in hotel, morning skate, room service lunch, leave for tour of city, supper at embassy. I laughed as I compared it to ours, which went something like: pick up breakfast at grocery store, morning run, cook lunch at hostel, leave for training, supper if you're lucky. When Jeff was in Prague at the World Championships as a reserve player, the hockey team paid to fly my sister over to spend the week with him. My husband isn't even allowed to come to practice, and if he comes to a Worlds, it is out of our retirement fund. I know major corporate sponsors, media attention, and the fact that they pull in tens of thousands of spectators are all far more impressive than our World Cup finals, where the hardly visible crowd is made up of family members and school groups. But is that any reason to let us sleep in the squalor of a Hungarian gymnasium before a World Cup?

To be honest, we were the ones who were duped into agreeing to stay there as a last-minute arrangement. The week earlier when we were at the training centre, we were feeling fine with all the luxuries of a superb cafeteria, free internet, and best of all, TVs in every bedroom! We realized that for the following week when we would be in Budapest, we needed to find a place for the five of us girls. That's when the Hungarian High Performance Director stepped in and told us he could get us an "apartment," complete with satellite TV for only 90 dollars per night in total. Unhesitating, we took it! When the minibus dropped us off in front of a school, we were slightly confused, but a woman rattling off in Hungarian came out and hustled us into the main hallway. She handed us about 37 keys and then beckoned us to follow her up four flights of stairs to our "bedrooms." Four walls around a few mattresses, and the room smelled like a gym bag. We smiled thinly and decided that we would immediately start looking for a new place.

But as much as we complain, we love what we do and what doesn't kill us only makes us better travellers. I dare any of those hockey players to try to survive on our budget! Thankfully, all that sort of stuff is taken care of at the Olympics, so I wouldn't be curled up in a sleeping bag in the stands of a stadium in Athens.

Modling, Austria.
May 1–3, 2004

I once again left Budapest regretfully. The regret didn't last, though, because we were soon on a train and heading west to Austria where the memories of last year's victory were fresh in my mind. I was in much better shape this year. I was almost completely injury-free, which is quite an accomplishment for my war-torn body. Last year at this same competition I had to ask Monique to tape up my ankle, which was just healing after a nasty sprain. Why was my teammate taping my ankle and not our team trainer, you ask? Considering that we did not even have a coach with us that time, we could hardly ask for our own trainer or doctor, so we had to rely on each other.

Being in better shape physically this year did not compensate for the fact that I was unfocused mentally. There is a clear difference between being lucid and in a state of over-thinking. Lucidity in sport is best understood in terms of a numb awareness. You are completely aware of what is going on around you, but you retain an ability to tune it out at any time. This state prevents you from getting annoyed or distracted should something go wrong. It's an emotional and intellectual state that makes athletes calm yet intense, and lets them learn, adapt, and correct problems in their performances instinctively and effortlessly. Learning to summon this state is called mental preparation and it is the bane of most athletes' existence. I know so many people who can win regularly in practice but they just can't pull it together for competition. As an observer, you just want to tell them, "Don't think!" but the brain always needs something to think about. So part of the trick is to replace the thoughts of panic and "whaddoo I do?" with a constructive plan.

My husband, Geordie, taught me this as I watched him prepare for his first-ever solo concert in Paris. Knowing that he was going to be the only one on stage with a couple of hundred people watching, I wondered if he was getting stressed out and where his focus was in these last few days of preparation. "What do you think about on stage?" I asked.

"My song," he replied with simplicity.

"You mean you don't think about how the performance is going, if it's going to be your best ever or even if people are enjoying it?"

"Well, I sort of sense if people are enjoying it because part of my job as a musician is to captivate the crowd, but I don't *think* about it. I don't have time! I am too busy thinking about what I need to do to get through this song. After the intro, I am thinking about my first verse and then I am thinking about the chorus, the second verse, the bridge, the chorus and the ending. When it's all over I take a few seconds to enjoy the applause or … whatever … and then I think about my next song."

If I were a man, I would be an Olympic Champion by now. Male simplicity (and by this I mean a man's penchant for focus) is a truly beautiful quality. There is nothing more frustrating than to look at the bathroom that I share with Geordie and compare his five toiletries with my fifty-five. It is difficult for me to separate what is truly needed and useful from what is just distraction. Tweezers? Truly needed and useful. Black-slanted, blue-pointed and silver-rounded tweezers? Distraction. Thinking about what I have to do to get through my next fencing match? Truly needed and useful. Thinking about whether this match is my best ever and whether I will win the whole competition? Distraction.

Since I was just coming off an injury the previous year in Modling, I knew that I had to keep my focus on what was truly needed and useful. On that day I had no energy to waste on stress, fear or over-thinking. All I could focus on was what was needed to get through my current match. The matches to follow would take care of themselves in their own time, and so I was focused on the present moment and it showed. I won each of my matches and ended up winning the whole tournament. It dawned on me that when you win a tournament, it's as though there's only a single victory, repeated again and again. Like in the movie *Groundhog Day*, minus the tedium. If you had told me I would be able to do that just after an injury I would have laughed.

This year in Modling, I had no injury to use to keep me focused. (For me, an injury keeps me focused on not wasting energy, observing my opponents, and doing the most efficient things possible to beat them.) I also had my coach and teammates to further distract me. Of course, this is all said with 20/20 hindsight. Had I won, the paragraph would go something like this: "This year in Modling I had no injury, so I was able to focus on my fencing and it was even more exciting because I had my coach and teammates there to support me." But this is all relative to the result and I lost for reasons that I alone know. I was cheated—no, seriously, I was distracted and unable to achieve that state of numb awareness that is the essence of excellence in athletics, and in everything, I believe.

In my second, and unfortunately last match of the day, I drew a Hungarian named Renata Fodor, whom I had beaten all that week in practice and in our mini-competitions. I was ahead by at least four points when somehow I started thinking about anything and everything except the match at hand. Could I win this World Cup for the second year in a row? Did I forget to turn off the oven? Wouldn't that be hilarious if her name had no "f"? When I woke up,

Renata had changed her tactic and caught up to me and we were going into sudden-death overtime! I looked around madly for help, asking Daniel, my teammates and even the 10-year-old Austrian boy keeping time, "What should I do? Help me!" Lucidity and awareness—hasty exit, stage left. Panic and doubt—flood the stage from all wings. My coach threw out some standard action for me to do, my teammate disagreed with him out loud and the Austrian boy just sat there blinking behind his round, blue-framed plastic glasses. You can imagine the scene that unfolded. She attacked, I froze. She hit, I watched. She yelled, I whimpered. She took off her mask and celebrated and I turned to the Austrian boy and wanted to shake him and scream, "Why didn't you tell me she was going to attack!" I certainly did get upset at my coach, but I was really mad at myself, and it had little to do with him. It was my lack of concentration, and only my own presence of mind could have solved that. Nobody can do that for me, no matter how good a coach that person is. It was a tough lesson, but a timely one, considering we were entering the last stretch of the World Cup season before the Olympics and I needed every epiphany I could get!

Legnano, Italy.
May 14–15, 2004

U nfortunately, fencing is probably the worst-managed sport in the world. It is certainly the only one I know in which the athletes have to pay but the spectators get in for free. The highest profit is garnered not from ticket sales, but rather from each athlete's entry fee. Free admission might encourage a higher turnout, but it certainly doesn't help the business side of the sport. Instead of being left with a neat profit, the poor host club of an average World Cup is left with a gymnasium full of broken weapons, banana peels and Gatorade bottles. Years of this have led to cost cutting and now nearly all World Cups are located well outside major European cities, in suburbs or villages where renting huge gym spaces costs less. For example, a competition would not be held in Paris, but in Saint Maur, the land of a zillion bakeries and a 45-minute train ride from downtown Paris. Another World Cup would not be held in London but in Ipswich, a slightly less cosmopolitan suburb a three-hour train, bus and taxi away (think *Coronation Street* but without the quaintness). Alas, this time the competition was not in Milan, but 50 kilometres away in Legnano, a provincial town where every teenager hates to live and every grandparent can't understand why.

Happily, I am getting older, so travelling to these little towns has become a pleasure, especially after the frenetic pace of Paris. In Paris, there are three speeds for moving on the streets: fast, faster and Parisian. Even if you are clipping along at a pretty good pace in the "walking lane" on escalators or moving sidewalks, you can expect that someone will clear his or her throat behind you or call out a crisp, "Pardon!" When we arrived at the airport in Italy, we tried to use all of our best travelling tricks to get to Legnano as efficiently as possible. In the past it has been a three-hour process of busing to Milan, taking the metro to the train station, and then a train to Legnano and a taxi to our hotel. This year, however, it looked like Team Canada's luck had changed. An elderly gentleman made a beeline for us as we exited the customs control with our conspicuous fencing bags. "Are you arriving from Holland?" he asked in French. We looked at him strangely, and after years of travelling in Italy we half expected to hear something like, "I can get you a cheap taxi to anywhere in Milan for the price of a few kisses and a slap on your ass, just follow my friend Guido down this dark alleyway …" Then again, he might just be a sweet old man. Turns out he was neither. When we said that we were arriving from Paris he looked irritated and asked if we had seen the International Fencing Federation Observer, "because I've been waiting here for well over half an hour, you know!" He was complaining about *his* travelling troubles to a group of Canadians? Boo hoo. Just as we were about to leave him, he threw us a bone. "Which hotel are you staying at?"

We smelled a free ride and put on our best smiles. "Albergo Al Corso," I replied in my best Italian accent and flashed him an endearing smile. "Oh, yes, I do know that one," he said, nodding knowingly and half closing his eyes as if he were already planning the route.

"So there are six of us, each with fencing bags, is that too much?" I asked hopefully.

"No, it should be fine …" he started and we all looked at each other thinking, "We are saved!" Then he continued, "But you will have to get two taxis because they won't take all six of you. See you at the competition!" He turned away from us and raised his limp wrist, waving only his fingers as he walked away. Our mouths were agape for the briefest moment before we snapped them shut and charged off to find our way. Having thought we were getting a ride, the idea of public transport had become unbearable. We decided to take taxis and ended up paying twice as much as we'd have paid for the bus, but for much less than half the hassle.

At the hotel, to avoid bickering over roommate choice ("Sherraine snores too much!" "Catherine is messy!" "Monique talks too much!" "Marie-Eve reads too much!"), we have developed a system for deciding roommates. First, we get the configuration of rooms (i.e., one double and a triple or two doubles and a single, et cetera), and the room numbers. Then we draw cards or roll dice. Whoever gets the lowest number stays in the first room and so on until the rooms are filled. Honestly, this system was created because we all really like each other and didn't want to create patterns of who stays with whom, so we thought random selection was the way to go. Daniel always laughs at us, and I am sure he has never seen a group of girls who get along so well.

The competition in Legnano was a surprising change from this year's pattern of second or third round loss ... I won the bronze medal! The best thing about getting into the medal round in Legnano is that Italians love their prizes. If you ever need extra give-away trophies, do well in Legnano and you will be set for a few years. I was awarded two gigantic cups, a plaque, a little partici-pation medal, flowers and a funky, green plastic bracelet. It really is a crapshoot with prizes at World Cups. Prize worth is no reflection on the strength of the competition with prestige but has entirely to do with the tournament's sponsors. For instance, two years ago the World Cup in Göteborg, Sweden, was sponsored by a computer company and the winner received a laptop! (This year in Göteborg, which of course was the year I made the medal rounds, the prizes were stainless steel candlestick holders. I am not complaining about my candlestick holders ... my mom really liked them. And let's face it, anything has to be better than the ribbon-less medal and Power Point flag-raising ceremony I received after winning the 2003 Grand Prix World Cup in Sydney, Australia.)

With the excess of prizes awarded, the trip home would be cumbersome but at least I was only taking a direct flight back to Paris, where I could put my trophies in my basement storage. But even taking my prizes home was somewhat tricky until one of my teammates came through for me. As happy as I was that Catherine offered to carry one of my cups through Malpensa airport, I must admit I was a little suspicious of her intentions when I saw her lovingly stroking the cup and whispering the words, "My Preciousssssssss." You see, over the last few years there has been a noticeable absence of trophies on the Alberta fencing circuit. My home province doesn't have the budget of the Italian Federation, so when you win a competition they engrave your name and the year of your victory on a small brass plate. This plate is then placed on the trophy which you are allowed to keep for one calendar year. Catherine, who is from Calgary, has been quite verbal in accusing me of having all of the Albertan trophies in my possession. Hoarded in my parents' basement, to be precise. Catherine argues that because I was probably the last person to have won all of the Alberta competitions, the trophies must be at my place. I asked her where she came up with this crazy idea and she said that the theory resurfaces every time an Alberta fencer wins a competition but goes home empty-handed.

"You guys honestly think that my mom has every Alberta trophy in her basement? For what purpose? Like she just polishes them and talks to them? Who is she, Gollum?"

Catherine laughed, but this was no joke! I had no idea my own dear Albertans could be thinking such things about me, and even worse, about my sweet, innocent mother!

Now in the airport I saw the envious look in Catherine's eye. She wanted that trophy. Not for herself, but for the glory of Alberta sports. "Okay," I told her after breaking her gaze by waving my hand in front of the trophy, "I will donate a trophy or two—"

"Or five," she countered.

I continued, "To replace those that have somehow disappeared from the Alberta circuit, through no fault of my own or my mother's."

This seemed to satisfy her and we made our way back to Paris with no further discussion.

Malaga, Spain.
May 21–23, 2004

S pain. The country of duels. Families avenging their honour in chivalrous sword matches. The place where "Crimes of Passion" is a category on work resumes. So why the gasping when I walked around town with my épée in hand? It was the first day of the individual competition and because I had a bye for that round, Daniel told me to come to the gym anyway and take a lesson with him. For a lesson I only use a mask, glove and sword, so I didn't see the sense in hauling my whole fencing bag to the gym in the tiring Spanish heat. I tucked my mask and glove under my arm, took my épée in hand and walked to the gym. Halfway there, I remembered that the entrance fee for a Grand Prix competition like this one was three times the regular price so I needed more money. The only bank I knew was the one by our hotel, so I hurried back, hoping that I could still make my lesson on time. The road was all uphill. To anyone watching me climb up I must have looked like a Musketeer doing the Stairmaster. Relieved, I walked into the serene, air-conditioned bank. Pulling out my bank card, I realized with a groan that there was no bank machine in the lobby, so I walked into the actual bank to ask where I could find the machine. Had my Spanish been better than that of a toddler, the situation might not have been so bizarre. I could have asked, "Will you be so kind as to point me in the direction of the closest automated teller?" However in my pathetic Spanish all I could say was, "Where is the money?" I repeated the question as I noticed three well-dressed tellers slowly but cautiously step away from me looking more than a little scared. They were all staring straight at my épée. It occurred to me that I had just walked into a bank brandishing a weapon and asking for money. It probably didn't help that their crown prince was getting married later that afternoon and Spain's national security had been ratcheted up.

"Nice sword," one teller said in perfect English, still watching for any false moves.

"Uh, thanks," I said and shyly put my épée behind my back as I reposed my question. She pointed to the left of where she was standing and I very slowly walked over and withdrew some cash.

My épée has caused some issues on the streets of Paris as well, although people are much more understanding and even make jokes out of it. On the Metro there was a homeless man walking through the car asking for money. When he came to where I was sitting he pulled back his open hand and looked from the épée to me and back to the épée. "What's that?" he asked with wide eyes.

"An épée," I answered.

"A *real* one?"

"Yeah, as real as they get nowadays."

"Wow! And you know how to use it?"

"Sure do."

"Well good luck to you, madame, and good luck!" he said with a flourish as he moved on to the next car.

To avoid this, I sometimes place my épée in a backpack with the tip poking out the top. Walking past Omar, the King of Hallal Chicken, who owns the chicken shop in our neighbourhood, there is sure to be a wisecrack. "Hey, Sherraine, you know that they now sell smaller cell phones than that, some with almost no antennas!"

"Yeah, I know, but you should see the reception I get with this guy!" and we laugh together.

After the Spanish bank episode was over, I relaxed a little more. Whatever extra we spent on the entry fee for the competition we saved in hotel costs. Daniel's buddy Pascal Petit-Jean had found us a cheap hotel that was within walking distance of the competition. We thought it strange that in such a touristy area as Marbella (the Malaga tournament is actually held in Marbella), the hotel could afford to charge so little. Finding the hotel wasn't a problem, as we had the address. Finding the reception desk proved a little more difficult. We double-checked the address and, yes, it was right. Monique offered to go ask at the hardware store and she came back smiling. "Wow! We can check in *and* stock up on sandpaper and superglue!" The hotel was managed by the hardware store and to downsize, the checkout till became the reception desk. While Monique was waiting for the key to her room she asked the clerk about the price of a piece of sandpaper. When the clerk realized that she was a guest of the hotel he said, "Oh, take it for free!" I guess they made up for not providing breakfast by handing out free sandpaper. Fencers have quite a tool kit for maintaining their gear, which always needs replenishing, and this hotel provided for all of our fix-it needs. I guess if you lost the room key it wasn't a big deal: you could just go to the front desk and they could cut you a new one. Pascal is friend and protector of the Hungarian National team and had arranged the same gig for them. While the Canadian team was delighted at how low our costs were for the weekend, the Hungarian girls didn't seem impressed. They explained that the federation was paying for their whole trip, so they weren't *too* excited at the prospect of sleeping in a bare, non-air-conditioned room next to a busy street. I understood their rationale. If our federation had been paying for us to sleep in that gymnasium in Budapest a month ago, I would have been miffed.

Even though it was the second-last team World Cup before the Olympics, the Hungarians were supposedly sent there with explicit instructions to relax and have fun. I guess when your team is consistently ranked in the top three in the world, "relax and have fun" means party all weekend and still manage to win the whole thing, because that is what happened. The girls spent the first half of their weekend in a pre-victory celebration with dinners out and late nights. We would hear them coming in as we were tucked into our beds like good little Canadians. We had an okay result, finishing tenth, but the Hungarians were outstanding, considering their antics. I don't have regrets about our preparation, because it's what we do, but this clearly shows that there is no precise formula for victory in high-level sports. Sometimes serious preparation is needed and other times I guess a little relaxation is what inspires the athlete to win.

Havana, Cuba.
June 18–20, 2004

The only disadvantage of living in Europe—besides having to go to five different stores to get groceries—is when World Cups happen in the Caribbean. The problem isn't the location, the heat or even the constant barrage of whistles and "psssts" from the entire male population. The problem that affects us most of all is that two neighbouring countries refuse to communicate with each other. Cuba and the United States are an endless source of frustration for those of us on the World Cup circuit.

I am no political analyst, but I know from personal experience that this has made many people's lives very complicated. Even with the two islands being only 1,765 kilometres apart, the back-to-back World Cups in Cuba and Puerto Rico have become a living nightmare. Usually, the World Cup calendar is set up to make travel as manageable as possible, especially with two tournaments on consecutive weekends: Switzerland–Italy, China–Taiwan, et cetera. You would think that Cuba–Puerto Rico seem reasonable, especially considering that they are only as far apart as Toronto and Halifax. Then you realize that because of long-standing political issues you cannot fly directly between the two countries.

Running With Swords

You cannot even fly through the USA to Cuba, so to avoid going back and forth from Europe to the Caribbean twice in one week, we would fly from Paris to Montreal and then from Montreal back and forth to Havana and Puerto Rico.

So, we made our yearly trek to Cuba and Puerto Rico. The trip sounds glamorous. A tropical paradise with some sparring on the side. Two different Caribbean beaches in two weekends! What a life it is to be an amateur athlete—but read on.

Most people know Cuba as a poor but stubborn and surprisingly contented nation. Most Americans refuse to admit that Cuba exists at all. I am of two minds on this subject. Being a relatively young traveller who went to the Eastern European countries of Hungary, Slovakia and the Czech Republic well after their Westernization, I have *never* been to a major city in any country where I have not been barraged with American culture. Especially visible is the influence of the Golden Arches. When that Iron Curtain came down, Ronald McDonald and Colonel Sanders ran on stage in a two-man Broadway show, setting up in train stations and airports the world over. For this reason, Cuba is refreshing. I first walked through Havana 10 years ago, and I remember thinking, "Why do I feel out of sorts? Surely the Tourist Disease isn't moving from my big intestine to my brain?" Then I realized that it was because there were no major American influences to be found. They don't even take American credit cards! Being Canadian and constantly having to clear myself as a non-American while travelling, I can appreciate this. It's the only foreign country where the locals naturally assume that people speaking English are Canadian.

Needless to say, the circuitous trip to Cuba was exhausting, but when we finally arrived at our hotel at 3:00 a.m., we were rewarded with a four-star, all-inclusive resort! There were bellboys eager to lug our fencing bags to our large, air-conditioned rooms that were 10 steps from the crystal clear ocean and a beautiful sandy beach. After the gymnasiums, youth hostels and rent-by-the-hour hotels we had stayed in during the past year, this was a paradise.

Sherraine MacKay

However, staying at a ritzy, all-inclusive resort puts you under an inordinate amount of pressure; you have to take advantage of everything! Experience and age helped keep me focused in a place like this. The difference between young athletes and mature ones is apparent in the level of alcohol use, time spent crisping up in the sun and the frequency of visits to the hotel disco. "It was my first experience with Cuban rum!" doesn't cut it with the coach once you are past the age of 19. On our orientation day, the tour guide, "Eduardo, at your service," started talking about the catamaran, disco, paddle boats, daily excursions and the rules about bringing back Cuban "friends" to the hotel room—and I zoned out, wishing I could just go back to the room and watch HBO. He got me back again, though, when he mentioned the word buffet. As much as you can eat three times per day? It was like the "Love Boat" had landed and I was invited on board. Forget experience and maturity, I just hoped I could still squeeze into my fencing pants by the end of the week!

Besides the constant temptation of gluttony, this fancy hotel had another drawback. It was located about a one-hour drive away from the competition and training venues. I know that there are always long bus rides at the Olympics, so I tried to tell myself that it was good preparation. Transportation training. But after 45 minutes of being jolted up and down in the backseat of a taxi with my sweaty skin sliding against that of my two teammates as our driver swerved left and right in vain efforts to avoid countless potholes, I hoped that this "training" was more intense than the real thing to come.

We finally arrived for pre-competition workout a bit dazed and dehydrated. We were not at all ready to put on our layers of protective gear and bounce around trying to hit each other in a non-air-conditioned gymnasium for two hours. As we walked in, we noticed that the Cubans weren't either. The whole national team was scattered about on the pistes, spread-eagle in complete silence. Either they were doing mental preparation or they'd all died of the heat. As we started jogging around the gym, the noise must have woken them and one-by-one they rose and started warming up.

We were not accustomed to training in excessive heat. Cubans, however, obviously had this down to a science. Observing the Cubans, I noticed that they just didn't sweat. In 35-degree Celsius heat, training in full swing, not one of them was nearly as wet as I was just walking into the gym! During one of my matches with Eimey Gomez, the Great Cuban Hope, who was their only female fencer qualified for the 2004 Olympics, I noticed that she stopped mid-match and took something from her coach. As I watched her put a pill in her mouth and gag it down, I thought, either their Cuban doping is very primitive or this could be something to combat the heat. So I pointed at her mouth and furrowed my brow in puzzlement. She made a panting gesture and waved her hand in front of her face to show that it was hot even for her. "Potassium," she wheezed. Man, if the natives need supplements to survive in this climate, how much more would I need them? So later, back at paradise, I stocked up on bananas, because I would rather eat my way to health than take a pill any day!

The three litres of water I had brought to training was quickly gone so I ventured out into the neighbourhood to find a grocery store. This proved more difficult than you would think because in socialist Cuba you won't find two or three competing grocery stores in the same neighbourhood. There are also virtually no signs. So, I just walked up to the first person I saw and asked. My Spanish is limited, as you know from the bank episode, so the fellow I'd asked obliged me by responding in impeccable English, saying that he wanted to go buy beer anyway, so he would walk me to the store. Inwardly, I groaned thinking this guy just wants to flirt with me. Keeping my guard up, we started off together to the grocery store. Then it began, "So where are joo from?"

"Canada," I answered, wanting to keep it short and sweet.

"Oh, Canada ees beautiful!" he exclaimed, right on track.

"Yes, I know. Cuba is beautiful, too," I said, trying to turn the conversation back toward him.

"Jes, ees true. What is your job een Canada?"

"I am an athlete, a fencer. *'Esgrima'*."

"Oh wonderfool! Joo must be bery strong!"

Then before he could hand out the string of compliments and finish with a marriage proposal, I quickly asked, "And what is your job?"

"I am a doctor," he replied. "A heart doctor. I know your country because I go for six months every year to study in Vancouber in a hospital for children. Right now, though, I need a beer because I just come from seeing a patient and I am angry."

"Why? What happened?" I asked, by now feeling quite foolish for not giving the guy a chance.

"My patient ees a young girl who has a genetic heart problem, but her parents say no to operation because of their releegion. Eet makes me so angry I say—excuse me for my words—'bastards, you are keeling your daughter.'" He looked at me sheepishly.

"It's okay, I understand it must be horrible to watch someone die when you could help them," I sympathized.

"Jes, and so I will go and try to calm down now. Here ees the supermarket." He pointed in front of us at some nondescript glass doors as we shook hands in farewell. "Good luck een your competition," he said kindly.

"Good luck in your job, and nice meeting you!" I waved goodbye, thinking how travelling helps you to mature, whether you want to or not. Mental note: don't jump to unnecessary and pessimistic conclusions. Someday, you may need a heart doctor and then where would you be, Little Miss "Everyone Wants to Hit On Me"?

As beautiful as our hotel may have been, it was not the "official" hotel selected by the competition, which meant that they were not "officially" obliged to inform us of any scheduling changes. Usually one of the perks of staying at the official hotel is that they have a shuttle bus come and pick you up a few hours before the start of the competition and any competition information is posted at the front desk. Well, at Hotel Copacabana we had hired a taxi driver to take us to the competition and the only thing posted at our front desk was "Salsa lessons at noon in the disco—Bring your own thong." The first day of competition—the qualification day—went off without a hitch ... apart from a two-hour delay when a monsoon hit the gym and the power went out. The girls cabbed 45 minutes to the competition venue while I, having already qualified for day two, was able to take it easy in the air-conditioned comfort of my room. At supper that night, Daniel told us that since the competition started at 11:30 a.m., we would be leaving at 8:15 a.m. to arrive at the gym by 9:00 a.m. Daniel prides himself on being the first one in the gym, thinking it gives him the advantage of choosing his spot and watching the others arrive on "his turf."

The World Cups are seldom male / female combined events. Only three of our eighteen World Cups are in conjunction with the men's event, so we rarely see a different coaching style from Daniel's. Over the past few years, we have grown accustomed to arriving hours and hours ahead of the competition start time, and we have started to think that this is how every team behaves. We were shocked to see the Canadian men's team having a leisurely breakfast at 7:30 a.m. when their competition started at 9:00 a.m.!

"Don't you start in an hour and a half?" I asked incredulously.

"Yeah," they said between bites, "but we only need an hour to warm up. No big whoop."

"Oh," I sniffed, "it seems pretty last minute to me." I thought of how Daniel would totally freak out and call us deadbeat athletes if we arrived at the gym only an hour before our first match.

Later that morning, we were on the road to the competition, chatting amicably with George our Cuban taxi driver. As we pulled up to the gym, Jurek, the Canadian men's coach, came running out to meet us. "You must hurry!" he said, out of breath. "They are holding the competition only until 9:05 for you to arrive!"

We all looked at Daniel accusingly. "What? We aren't supposed to start until 11:30?! We have another two-and-a-half hours!"

"No, you only have five minutes because they changed the schedule last night and it was posted at the official hotels," Jurek explained.

When we translated it into French for Daniel, we watched him turn white with shock, then red with anger as he stormed in to "discuss" the matter with the organizing committee. I don't know if he was trying to buy us a few more minutes of warm-up time or if he just felt like yelling at someone. In any case, it didn't change anything because the competition was nearly underway.

As we walked into the gym, we didn't hear any of the standard clash and clang of blades because everyone had already completely warmed up and were just waiting for the match to be called. It is no exaggeration to say that a hush fell as we entered the gym. Seeing as this was—hopefully—a once in a lifetime occasion, I took the time to observe people's reactions to our blunder.

There were a few girls who were so focused on themselves that they didn't even take time to look up. Others, like the Hungarians (a really nice group of girls), looked at us questioningly and mouthed the words, "Are you okay?" The Italians giggled sympathetically. "Where have you been?" asked Imke Duplitzer halfway between concern and laughter.

"Oh, we already did our warm-up—on the beach!" I said as I went off to change into my fencing pants and jacket.

I decided to laugh too; if I became upset about the situation, I would not be able to concentrate on my first match, which was against Zuleidis Ortiz-Fuente, Cuba's 1997 World Championship silver medallist.

Because there are only ever four to eight pistes for more than one hundred fencers, competitions always stagger the start times of matches. This time I was among the very first few matches called on piste. So there I was, zipping up my jacket when I heard, "First call, MacKay, Canada, against Ortiz, Cuba, on piste two." I hurried over to the piste with my untied shoelaces whipping around my ankles. As I got there, a very kind Russian fencer, Oksana Jermakova, waved me over and said, "Be careful of piste, it is wet from humidity and you can fall. I warmed up there and it is little bit dangerous." I looked up to see where the water was coming from and, sure enough, I could see the moisture collecting on the ceiling and dripping right onto the piste. Between the bird poo and water falling onto the pistes, this competition was a recipe for injury. I mentioned it to the judge and he called over a cleaning woman to fix the situation. She brought a filthy, sopping mop with her and pushed around the water on the piste. This absolutely defeated the purpose of cleaning it up, but she seemed to think that she was helping and Ortiz seemed to take these sub-par conditions in stride, so I thought, "Who am I to argue?" and got en guard.

Since our van had pulled up and we had been told the disastrous news, Daniel had been in the office of the organizing committee arguing and pleading that they allow us more warm-up time. His reasoning was that it was simply unfair that we be denied the time, and their reasoning was that we would have had it had we stayed at the official hotel, not the Copacabana all-inclusive beach resort. Words were thrown back and forth, with Daniel often leading with his favourite phrase, "Never in my life …" He finally ran out of arguments, so he came beside my piste and told me to warm up. "Do some lunges, some stretching. Do some sprints in place. Do some high jumps to get your heart rate going." He looked so panicked that I felt I needed to calm *him* down. "Don't worry coach, I am okay. It will be all right!" I knew that it would be okay for two reasons. First of all, I really like to fence against Ortiz. She has a good style for me and I was pretty confident that I could win the match even without a warm-up. And even though "never in his life" had Daniel arrived two minutes before the start of a match, for me it was old hat. In fact, once I even arrived well after the match had begun.

We were at the World University Games in Beijing back in 2001, and having just gotten married two weeks prior, I turned the competition into something of a honeymoon. Instead of staying in the Village with the rest of the athletes, the coaches gave me once-in-a-lifetime permission to stay with my husband in a hotel a few blocks away. I was still expected to attend all the team meetings and functions which I did willingly. I even arranged to eat breakfast with my teammates in the Athletes' Village the morning of our team event.

I walked to the Athletes' Village listening to my Walkman, pausing every few minutes to bend at the waist and let the screaming abdominal pains course over my body. I had been horribly sick over the past few days, and I couldn't hold anything down. I wasn't confident at all that I could fence. Mulling this over on my way to the Village, I heard over the sound of my music a "slap, slap, slap" coming from behind me. I turned around to see my panicked husband sprinting toward me in his flip-flops and pyjama shorts.

"Sherraine! You've got —" he paused to catch his breath, "to get —" another gasp for air, "to the Village fast, because they are waiting for you."

"Yeah, I know," I said wondering why he was freaking out. "We are going to have breakfast in a few minutes."

"No, they are coming to get you in a taxi because the competition started half an hour ago! The other girls are already fencing!"

They had changed the schedule, and the only way Canada found out about it was through our physiotherapist who arrived early at the venue and heard the teams being called. He stalled for time as the Canadian girls were hustled out of their beds and sent directly to the competition site to fence against Estonia. Their instructions were clear: "Keep the score as low as possible and stretch out each match as long as you can. That will give Sherraine a chance to arrive and we will have a complete team." As flattered as I was to hear that they were waiting for me, I was in no shape to be anyone's saviour. I doubted whether I could make it through a whole match without stopping for vomit breaks. Because I had intended to go to the Village for breakfast, I had left all my equipment in the vacant Village bedroom that had been assigned to me, but in our rush to get to the venue, my fencing stuff was left behind. So the scene looked something like this: three-quarters of the team arrived barely in time to start the match; half an hour later, I show up; ten minutes later, my equipment shows up and I'm on the piste fencing the last match.

As it turned out, I didn't have to be anyone's saviour because Marie-Eve Pelletier, Marina McConkey and Magda Krol had done such a good job of keeping the score painfully low that the Estonians were ahead only 16 to 14 going into the last match. Normally, by this point, the overall score should be around 40, so you can appreciate what a defensive game my teammates had played. After a few courtesy warm-up lunges, I hooked up to the piste and readied to fence against the last girl. I tied it up as the time ran out, and then we were bound for sudden-death overtime. I told my rebellious stomach to behave as I focused on getting the last hit. There was no way that I wanted anyone to blame our team loss on my honeymoon, so I was desperate to win. I pushed her into the end of the piste and she hesitated just before attacking me. I saw her coming and moved out of the way, hitting her as she came in. I tried to celebrate by jumping up and down with my teammates, coaches and Team Canada officials, but my stomach said "not so fast" and I ran off in search of the bathroom.

I'd established myself as a world-class last-minute fencer. I even wondered if I could pad this reputation, and save my late appearances for critical matches to inspire fear.

I would need to draw on that special talent here in Cuba against Ortiz. As I got en guard, I had only one thought: focus on the fencing. There were other thoughts flashing through my mind,

S h e r r a i n e   M a c K a y

like, "I hope she doesn't mind losing to someone who has had 20 seconds of warm-up," but I pushed those thoughts out of my mind and zoomed in on the match before me. And I won!

Actually, it was fairly easy to warm up in the excessive Cuban heat. Just breathing made you sweat. As I was sitting on a chair waiting for my next match to be called I saw my opponent, Andrea Rentmeister, from Austria, walk past me and stop at the wall. She was poised as if she were going to pounce on something. She was behaving so oddly that I felt no shame whatsoever in asking her what on earth she was doing.

"I'm trying to catch him!" she whispered and took a step closer to the wall. "But do you think he is poisonous?" Now I was really curious so I looked closer, and there beside my bag pressed up against the glass window was a frog about the size of my palm. Then I saw the light bulb appear above Andrea's head as she pointed her finger in the air and said, "Aha!" She tore over to her bag and returned with a piece of material. "We can trap him in this!" she said as she handed me the material.

"We?" I thought. "Now she has me involved in Operation Frog Rescue? I'm just trying to relax before my match in a few minutes … against her!"

So in true Laura Ingalls Wilder style, we chased after this little frog until I trapped him in the cloth, and then we set him free in a small creek beside the venue. Once he had hopped a few times and we were certain we had not maimed him in the catch, Andrea and I looked proudly at each other and then went into the gym and waited for our match to be called. The match was fairly close, but I won and moved into the third round to take on Imke Duplitzer.

I enjoy fencing against Imke because at least I know that the match will be a rip roarin' free-for-all. There is no chance of getting bored because we are both attackers. Imke loves to attack, and I love to counter-attack; thus, our matches always fall into the most exciting patterns: lunge, lunge, score. Lunge, flèche, score, and so on, until, in about three or four minutes compared to the standard nine minutes, our match is over, and one of us is doing a victory yell. Neither of us ever dominates the other, so it always makes for

Running With Swords

an interesting match. This time was no exception, and it was my turn to be the winner. I moved into the quarter-finals against the Russian Anna Sivkova.

The match began in my favour. I was ahead by a few hits and she looked to have no idea of what to do. Then she pulled out a few tricks and threw me off my game. She started doing kamikaze attacks, and I was so shocked that I didn't react in time. Anna was too strong for me that day, winning by a couple of points. I would finish fifth overall. After the match I was sitting glumly by my bag when Anna's teammate, Karina Aznavourian, came over to talk with me. Months earlier she had asked me to buy some medicine for her that you can only get in France. It was for her coach, whose baby was not well. She sat down and thanked me again for helping her and her coach.

"It's really no problem, honestly!" I reassured her.

"Are you sure I can't pay you anything?" she asked.

"No, it is really inexpensive, and I don't mind at all!"

"Well, anyway, I have something to say thank you." She rushed off to her fencing bag and came back holding a brown paper bag. "It's for you and your husband," she said as she pressed it into my lap. It was a bottle of "Parliament Genuine Best Russian Vodka." Now it was my turn to thank her profusely. She shook her head, brushing off my thanks. "It's nothing, really ... although it is genuinely the best Russian vodka." I slipped it unopened into my bag and thought of how in any other "workplace" that exchange would be illegal. The fencing world really is an odd network of friends and colleagues.

I packed up my bag and reflected on the day. I had achieved that numb awareness I've told you about and had won most of my matches. I had remembered my past mistakes and corrected them quickly. This is, I guess, what they call "maturing" as an athlete.

Carolina, Puerto Rico.
June 26–27, 2004

Puerto Rico is home to my favourite judge of all time. He is not the best judge of all time, as he makes painfully obvious mistakes every so often, but he will always be my favourite. The relationship between athletes and judges is tricky. As an athlete, you want to be polite to your judge so that they know that you respect them. This prevents them from throwing their weight around and bossing you into submission. However, you don't want the relationship to progress from politeness into the "friendship" category: it's dangerous to become friends with a judge. If you do and they end up judging one of your matches, they subconsciously feel the need to prove to anyone who happens to be watching that they aren't favouring you. They end up treating you worse than they would if you had never smiled at them in the first place.

According to the creed of sport, athletes should decide who wins and who loses by their play alone. The judges' role is to prevent rule infractions that can affect the outcome of a match. Basically, he is like a daycare worker. He doesn't spend one-on-one time playing with one child, but lets the children play together and solves any problems that arise. In épée, undue judge influence happens less frequently because of the more objective nature of the rules, but in the 2003 World Cup in Cuba, I was one of its rare victims. I was against Anna Sivkova in the quarter-finals. The victor would move into the medal rounds. My judge was a very nice man from Puerto Rico. Over the previous year or so we had several conversations about the World Cup in Puerto Rico, the weather, and his daughter who was going to school in the United States. Then, that relationship came back to bite me. As nice as he was, I couldn't help myself from getting angry when, at a crucial time in the course of the match, he gave Anna a point even though she was clearly off the piste. The rules state that if a player leaves the field of play, her point is annulled, but there he was awarding her a point anyway. I was furious after the match. Anna apologized and said that she got lucky on that point. Luck? Luck has to do with lottery numbers, not points awarded illegally! But there was no sense crying over it again so I walked over to my chair shaking my head.

Just as I was about to sit down, my Puerto Rican friend walked by. At the same time as I was telling myself to shut up and let it go I couldn't resist reiterating once more that he had made a mistake. "Excuse me, you know that your call was a bad one and you made a mistake, don't you?" I never said I was the most polite person on the circuit, and at the time I had even less control of my tongue. What reaction was I after? Anger, sarcasm, some sort of righteous indignation? I had no idea, but I certainly didn't expect humility, which was what I was greeted with. "I know. I made a mistake. Mistakes happen sometimes and I am sorry." My mouth moved but nothing came out. I couldn't believe it. Someone was admitting he did something wrong?

Remember, I was living in France, a country of people who don't know how to spell "sorry" let alone say it. Many times in that country I have seen somebody knock something down in a store, and when a store worker comes over to clean up, there is no apology offered. The offender's presence at the scene of the accident is held to be tacit admission of guilt. Nobody in France seems to mind this, but for Canadians, this is unheard of! The first three words we learn in any foreign language are "yes," "no" and "sorry." Further, we apologize for things that are not our fault. When someone runs into me in the Metro, I instinctively say, "Pardon!" The person at fault usually waves a hand like, "It's okay, you little Canadian country bumpkin, I can deal with your back-woods ineptitude." Maybe I am reading too much into things, but lately I have walked away from those situations feeling dirty, like I took the blame for their rudeness.

Now here I was in Cuba and my judge was apologizing for his error. It was pretty phenomenal. His apology made my incessant complaining seem childish and pointless, which of course, it was. Obviously it's true: we all make mistakes. I made many in my match that day, which is why I didn't win, so how could I ask my judge to be perfect? Since that time he has earned my admiration for his humility and honesty, which are rare in sport and in the world at large.

So this year I went off to the Puerto Rican World Cup happy that I was going to a place in which such fine human beings as my friend the judge could be found. I was doubly happy because Puerto Rico is the only tournament that gives out cash prizes! Good ones! If any of you reading this start to laugh when I tell you the amount of cash given to the winner, you are obviously used to watching golf, where the Masters winners take home over one million American dollars! Remember, fencing is a low-profile sport, and if you gave us a hot water kettle as a prize we would go home smiling. The winner of this World Cup went home holding an envelope fattened with twelve hundred dollars in American cash!

This year the competition was even smaller than usual, which boded well for my chances at the cash. (Please don't read an obsession with money into all this talk. If money were an obsession, I would certainly not be fencing!) Due to the small numbers, I had a bye in my first round. This was nice because I could save my energy for the more intense matches at the end of the day. I won my first match against an American fencing in her first ever World Cup. She just seemed excited to be there and the match was over with no great surprises. After that, I faced a Chilean girl, Maria Ramirez, and I won decisively as I made my way closer to the first-place envelope.

The most important match of the day was my next one because the winner moved into the prize round. Julie Leprohon and I were called to battle it out on the piste. We fought hard, but I was stronger that day and won. My next match was against Imke Duplitzer! For the second weekend in a row I came up against her, and for the second weekend in a row I came away victorious! During our match, there was a horrific storm and I could barely hear the judge over the pounding rain on the roof. I waited for the electricity to cut out at any time, putting our match on hold. However, the match went off without a hitch.

As the rain continued, I was called to the piste for my last match. For the twelve hundred dollars—I mean the gold medal— I had to fence against Claudia Bokel, another great German fencer. This match was my closest all day, and it went into sudden-death overtime. It was the highest-paying point I have scored in my life and with the win my student loan was that much closer to being paid off! Besides the obvious thrill of winning money, winning that competition was a nice way to end that World Cup season. I had not won any other events that year and only medalled in two, so I was feeling doubtful about my ability to perform in two months' time at the Athens Olympics. This World Cup gave me the taste of victory once again. I never feel such satisfaction and elation as I do when I win a World Cup, and I could take this feeling with me all the way to the Olympics.

Pre-Olympic Training Camps in Ovronnaz, Switzerland.
July 3–August 10, 2004

The final stage had begun. All the World Cups were finished and we had entered the "make or break" period. Daniel always says that an entire year can be made or broken in the last month of training prior to the Olympics. To prove that he is, of course, always right, he scheduled three entirely different training camps throughout July and into August. Because the Athletes' Village is located in the hills surrounding Athens, our first camp involved 10 days of altitude training in the serene Swiss mountains. Because Athens is polluted, we would do 10 days of smog training in grey Paris. Finally, because Athens is bloody hot, we had 10 days of training scheduled on the dry, crusty border between France and Spain. All of this could have been avoided by just going to Greece to train, but I wasn't about to be the one to tell the emperor that he was parading around without any clothes. Realizing that there are many cultural clashes that can occur between a team and a coach from different backgrounds, we have changed our team motto from "Go Canada Go" to "Don't Think Aboudit."

For a group of Olympians, we were a pretty pathetic sight as we all met to travel to our first training camp in Switzerland. The meeting was scheduled first thing in the morning on the outskirts of Paris where Daniel was waiting for us in the 11-passenger rental van. We were all exhausted for some reason. "We" included the Canadian National Women's Épée team, composed of Julie Leprohon, Monique Kavelaars, Catherine Dunnette and me. "We" also included the Algerian National Women's Épée team, or Zahra Gamir; the Colombian National Women's Épée team, or Angela Espinosa; and last, but not least, the Venezuelan National Men's Épée team, consisting of Silvio Fernandez. It is fairly common to share training camps because everyone is always searching for someone to spar with. Not many countries have a great depth of strong fencers to ensure that training camps are challenging and a place where members can train against diverse styles (Russia, Hungary, Germany and France are a few such exceptions).

Our guests were all foreigners who lived and trained in Paris and needed some sparring partners leading up to the Olympics. The last World Cup of the season had taken place about a week earlier in Puerto Rico, and most of us had flown more or less directly from there. In the few days between the tournament and the training camp, Silvio had taken some time for a quick trip to his home in Venezuela to do some pre-Olympic media schmoozing. He had it all planned out: he'd first be his country's flag bearer, then minister of sport, and finally president of the country. I guess he thought a good media image was the first step to such an illustrious career. On the other hand, Angela had been given an International Scholarship to attend a training camp in Los Angeles, so she had spent a few days in the City of Angels before flying home to the City of Lights. Monique had been wearing a big diamond on her left hand for some months now, so she took a few days for a quick trip down the aisle, and the rest of the Canadian team took those same few days to enjoy it! Living in Paris has posed a lot of logistical problems for Monique's love life. When they were dating, her hockey-player boyfriend lived in Chicago. They became serious and he wanted to live closer to her so he signed with a team in Switzerland, only a four-hour train ride away. They got engaged and then he signed with a team in Sweden, so like it or not, beginning in September they would be living in the land of the 10:00 a.m. sunrise. A wedding was inevitable, but now the travel was even more complicated. Should she plan her marriage to take place outside of our competitive season and during his, or should she tack it onto the World Cups that took place in the Western Hemisphere, when we would have no excuse to miss it and neither would the groom? She decided to get married right after Puerto Rico and I must say it was very conveniently planned right before our training camp, so we could feel free to eat as much cake as we wanted!

When he arrived in Paris, Silvio was tired from all the interviews he gave during the short time he had spent in Venezuela. Angela was tired from the time change between Los Angeles and Paris. We were tired from all the partying at Moe's wedding, and Zahra is just *always* tired. Monique had the best excuse of all … post honeymoon fatigue. She arrived in Paris with a fencing bag full of gifts, a smile full of contentment and a cellphone full of credit to call her new husband. Needless to say, the car ride to Switzerland was a very restful six hours with only one toilet break and a lot of rhythmic snoring. It is good that Daniel didn't rely on our scintillating conversation to keep him alert since our silence would have put even God to sleep. We arrived in Ovronnaz right on time for supper. After a hearty meal, I was off to bed because the next morning Daniel had scheduled my fencing lesson for 6:00 a.m. As painful as it may sound to wake up at the crack of dawn and be alert enough to hit someone accurately and rapidly, it was, in fact, the easiest part of our daily schedule. After my lesson there was physical training, weight training, speed training, power training, balance training—and oh, yeah, fencing training. I know it might seem like a lot, but honestly, time flew and everyone was very motivated whether it was by the upcoming Olympics or by the Beyoncé music in the background, so we gave it everything, constantly pushing each other to live up to the Olympic creed of "Higher, Faster, Stronger!"

Running With Swords

Daniel had thought of everything when he planned this training camp … even our break time. Museums, shows, picnics, he planned it all! Of course, to prevent our minds from swaying the slightest bit away from sport, he had carefully chosen an athletic theme for each fun outing. Our day trip was to the Olympic Museum in Lausanne. It was truly phenomenal, with displays of the torches and medals from each and every modern Olympics. The museum provides explanations about how the Olympics came to be and compares the modern Games to the Ancient Games. When our guide explained that the athletes competing in the Ancient Games would participate naked, we had to laugh. She explained that this was a measure to prevent women from disguising themselves and participating. We couldn't help cringing at how painful and ugly naked fencing would be, whether you were a man or a woman. Ouch!

If you go downstairs, you can watch any existing video of the medal matches throughout Olympic history. Just choose your event and press play to be instantly transported back to the Olympics of whatever year you wish. I had been at this museum a year earlier with Ernest Lamon, whose daughter Sophie was on the Swiss team when they won the silver medal in Sydney. It was pretty phenomenal to think that she and her teammates were recorded in the Olympic archives. Quite an achievement for a 15-year-old!

It is often easier to be impressed with other people's achievements than your own. You are so close to the situation that you forget how remarkable it is to outsiders. This usually occurs to me whenever the Winter Olympics roll around. Watching TV, I see a friend of a friend competing in her event and I am shaking with excitement, telling everyone around me that, "I know someone who knows that athlete—isn't that something? Oh, I hope she does well!" So when I instinctively downplay the fact that I am going to compete in the biggest athletic show on earth, I realize how pretentious it must look to those who are shaking with excitement for me.

On the top floor of the museum I was finally able to have an appreciation for my own participation in the Olympics. There was another archive and even though I hadn't won a medal, I was a part of this one. The museum has installed about six computers to find and display information about every athlete that has ever competed in the modern Olympic Games regardless of the result. I was standing there researching with Angela and Silvio. Angela and I had both competed in the Sydney Olympics in 2000 and we looked up our own names, giggling at the fact that we were a part of the Olympic archives.

We knew that Athens was going to be Silvio's first Olympics so we teased him when he punched in his name searching for his Olympic track record. "You're well known, Silvio, but you've got to compete before they will enter your name, silly!"

"Voila!" he said as he stepped back from the computer where sure enough, there was his name, *Silvio Fernandez*.

"Whoa, that's wild." Angela and I leaned in a little closer and saw that beside his name was written, *Fencing, 1968, Mexico City*. We looked at each other, momentarily perplexed.

Silvio sighed as a teacher might when the students are inept at understanding the most basic of principles. "This is my father," he said patiently.

"Yeah," he said, "I would pester my mom constantly that I wanted to join the fencing club where my dad was the coach but he wouldn't let me because he said I was too small."

I looked up at his six-foot-three frame and shook my head, "Boy, I bet he is proud of you, now, eh?"

"Yeah. Apparently he can't stop telling people that I am going to the Olympics. He's coming to watch as a matter of fact. All the way from Venezuela."

While we were chatting about his dad's travel, Angela was working away busily on the computer screen. Finally, she found what she was looking for and her hands just fell by her sides in limp satisfaction. I peered at the screen and there was another Espinosa but with *Football, 1972, Munich* written beside it. I looked up at her to ask her who this was.

Running With Swords

"It was my father," she said simply, tears rolling down her cheeks.

We stood there feeling more than we could comfortably express. Angela's dad had died suddenly of a heart attack the previous summer a few weeks before the Pan American Games. She was living in Paris and she couldn't afford to fly home for a special trip, so she waited until after the Pan Am Games to return. Courageously, she competed in the Dominican Republic only days after her father's death before going home to be with her family in Colombia for a while. "My dad would have wanted me to do my sport so I will give my best in spite of how terrible I feel," she had told me when we talked just after she heard the news. I still don't know how she maintained her composure throughout the whole day of competition, but she did it. Now, in the Olympic Museum, as Angela stood there looking at her father's name recorded forever in the chronicles of sport, I realized how cross-generational and cross-cultural the Olympic Games truly are. I have never felt prouder to be part of such an event.

When I take into account the incredible people I have gotten to know through fencing, I can easily count all the tough training hours as worthwhile. Angela is one of those people. At age 26, she moved to Paris from Colombia with her fiancé and nothing else. No job, no friends, no understanding of the language. She has since learned to speak French beautifully, started university, gotten married to her fiancé and qualified for the Athens Olympics. Over time we have become quite good friends. She is the epitome of giving everything on the piste but not getting personal. She trains hard and will beat anyone she can but she always plays well within the rules and has a genuine smile for her opponent after the match, win or lose. At her Paris wedding (she had a big family one in Colombia, of course, in December 2005), at the end of October 2004, she had two bridesmaids. One was me and the other was Catherine Bravo, a fencer from Chile whom Angela had to beat to qualify for the Olympic Games in Athens. I mused that only exceptional people have the grace to become friends with those who could have been bitter rivals. Only people who chase goodness instead of greatness can make adversaries into friends.

Before we left the computer terminals at the Olympic Museum, I had one last thing to check. Over the past year I had run into a strange but engaging man on the bus from my Paris Metro stop to the National Training Centre, where I teach English lessons. Because this bus is the only public transportation that passes in front of the National Training Centre, there are always loads of athletes riding it. Among the athletes is a withered old man who always sits in the same seats reserved for pregnant women and war veterans. You can quickly guess which of the two he is as he tells his life story to anyone who happens to be sitting in front of him. Other people might cringe and sit elsewhere but I absolutely love this guy who adds such life to a bus full of dead-beats reading or listening to their Walkmans.

"Are you a sportsperson?" he asks in a stage whisper when you sit down in front of him.

He listens quickly to your answer before plowing on, this time at full volume, "I am a sportsperson!" He hesitates and looks around sheepishly like he is waiting for someone to say, "You're too old to do sports, grandpa!" and he corrects himself, "Well, I was."

"Really?" I say with feigned surprise, having heard it all before on last week's bus trip. I try to see if this guy's answers change from day to day or if he manages to keep them somewhat consistent. "In what discipline?"

"Track, 100 metre and 200 metre to be exact." Same answer as last week. "I competed in the 1928 Amsterdam Olympics. Do you know why I picked track?" he asks with a giggle. "To run after the girls! And I caught them, too!" he says triumphantly. "Now I don't go as fast, of course …"

The conversation slows down and I take a sip of coffee from my thermos. "Is that whisky?" he asks with a twinkle in his eye. I shake my head no, but offer him some nonetheless. He declines by raising his palm toward me. "Did you know that I was a parachutist fighting against Hitler? That's right, I fought with the French army in the Second World War. We would parachute right into the girls' arms!" He has me until the girls' arms bit and now I grow doubtful of everything he says. Sensing this, he pulls out a photograph. It's an old black-and-white with tattered corners and, sure enough, there he is in his military uniform. You hold it up to compare it to him and you notice he is wearing a winged military pin from many years ago. "Oh, I bet your heart skipped a beat when you saw that photo, eh?" he says.

"Actually, you do look a lot like a young Marlon Brando in this picture," I say. But, this alleged former Olympian is French, and not flattered by comparisons to celebrities.

He scoffs at me. "Ha! Only better!"

At this point I have only to agree and as the bus pulls up to the last stop I ask his name.

Gilbert Auvergne. I typed it into the computer and waited for the screen to flash the "not found" message we were confronted with when we typed in the name "Elvis Presley" to make sure it worked.

Gilbert Auvergne. 100 metre, 200 metre, 1928, Amsterdam. I froze. I couldn't believe it. He was telling the truth. Every week I had travelled on Bus 112 with a 90-year-old World War II veteran and Olympian who was full of more life and optimism than many of the 20-year-old athletes I trained with every day. The Olympics continue to astound me and I am learning to appreciate what they do for the lives of so many people.

Now in Ovronnaz our training began in earnest—sprints, weights, lessons and sparring—until it came time for another break. This time it was a picnic. We had no idea what to expect besides having to hike up a mountain to get to our picnic site. It was the most basic of incentives: if you want lunch, you'd better follow the mountain goats up this skinny trail to an elevation of three thousand metres. But this far into such a tough training camp, we were pretty much only responsive to rewards of food, so we nodded and started hiking. The man in charge of the sports centre, nicknamed "Yves the Hunter," had kindly offered to prepare a picnic for us at the top of the mountain.

Now, I have been to many picnics and I know they can range from a sandwich on a park bench to gourmet spreads on a checked cloth but never have I seen a picnic served on real plates with cutlery and glasses on a 20-foot banqueting table. Yves had prepared a four-course meal of appetizers, steaks and chicken breasts, roasted potatoes, salads, some delicious wine and wonderful dessert. We knew he ran the show well at the training centre but being able to put this together on a mountainside was worthy of an Olympic medal!

When it started to rain on our mountaintop picnic, we moved the banquet into the stables nearby, which were empty because the cows were out grazing. At first I balked at the coaches' suggestion of moving the tables inside the stable, but then I remembered that I was in Switzerland and their stables were probably cleaner than our parliament buildings. And I was right. Not only were they spotless and fresh smelling, the shepherds had named each stall to identify the sleeping cattle. Hugette, Sylvie and Ursula were the most prominent names on the stalls and were probably the shepherds' favourites. We lingered in the dim stable until the rain ended, and then made our way down the mountain in less than half the time it took to come up. Yves and the coaches cleaned up the picnic and we went home for a nap!

Yves took amazing care of the centre and of us. Switzerland is a strange country where they take people at their word and believe in the "honour system." At the Swiss training centre, the whole snack bar worked on this code, and it was nice to see how, given the opportunity, the people in our group went above and beyond being honest. "Well, I *thought* about having a Snickers bar, so should I just pay half?"

We did a lot of our training with music to help keep us going from 6:00 a.m. to 5:00 p.m. My coach had scheduled an individual lesson with me every morning, and I would purposely arrive earlier than him so I could turn the radio to the "old classics" stations, sit back and watch the comedy act unfold. Daniel would get a little misty-eyed when he heard the Bee Gees and then puff up his tail feathers telling me how he was the best slow dancer of his time. At 6:00 a.m. I need a laugh like that! In case I was a little low on energy, I would wait for the daily horoscope at 6:15.

When it comes to fencing, Daniel is an extremely focused individual who works harder than anyone I have ever met, but over time I have noticed two things that disturb his concentration: beautiful women and horoscopes. Maybe he is always listening to his horoscope to see if a beautiful woman will come walking into the gym. I think that in the past few years I have had more beautiful women pointed out to me than at any other time in my life, even more than during co-ed high school basketball trips. Back in Paris at the Racing Club, more often than not our lesson will have a 20-second break as Daniel waves coyly to one of the moms in the club coming to pick up her child. I have developed an automated playback response of "Oui, Maitre" to his "Wow, Sherraine, don't you think she is a beautiful woman?" If I am not in the mood to play along and he notices this, he'll throw in a courtesy, "but not as beautiful as you ..." as if that is supposed to make me swoon.

One morning at the training camp it was especially hilarious because Daniel's horoscope told him "today will be a great day of communication and problem-solving between you and your spouse." Daniel's wife was in another country, but I guess with all the time he is away from his family he takes comfort in anything. We all do at this point. Monique was anxious to see her new husband, and I was dying to see Geordie. These are the hard parts of high-level sport.

Whatever I missed in family during this camp was made up for in fans. Our training centre was also hosting a children's football (soccer) camp at the same time we were there. These were Swiss children aged eight to eleven: the hero years! I can remember being that age and assuming people became cooler as a natural consequence of getting older. Anyone 12 and up was totally hip. I guess this mentality is alive and well in Switzerland because these kids were awestruck that these adults with swords were going to the Olympics. To reward them for their good behaviour during the week, Yves had scheduled an autograph session for them. I had signed autographs for kids before. Whenever I talk to groups of Canadian children they always want me to sign something, whether it is their T-shirts or a scrap piece of paper just pulled from a binder.

So now in Switzerland I was ready for the attack. We were seated behind tables, which I assumed would serve to protect us as Yves opened the door and the kids came streaming in with wild eyes and blank paper. Swiss fencer Sophie Lamon had her own stack of photos that she gave away on a regular basis, which was one of the perks of being an Olympic medallist. The rest of us just used pieces of paper. Ninety kids cycled through the factory line of athletes. As they walked up and said only a, "Hello, madame. Sign here, please, madame. Thank you, madame," I was thinking, "What sort of abnormal children are these?" I had never seen kids so unerringly polite. Near the end of the session, however, they started to loosen up. When they started saying things like, "He thinks you're cute! Can you give me your phone number? Can I have a kiss?" I knew that underneath all those impeccable manners stood the same children you find anywhere, kids who just want attention however they can get it!

At the end of the 10 days, we all agreed that Daniel and the Lamon family had organized our best-ever training camp. The food was excellent, the staff was helpful, and there was a perfect blend of work and fun. As we drove back into the grey smog of Paris, we realized that the pristine mountain setting in Switzerland hadn't hurt a bit, either.

Paris, France.
July 15–July 17, 2004

Our second training camp was not quite as exciting or as enjoyable. This was part of the "work" of being an athlete. The camp had been organized with my home club located in the heart of Paris. The week before we arrived, however, the bosses had made a last-minute decision to completely renovate the club which left us with no place to train. While we were quietly chanting, "Swit—zer—land, Swit—zer—land" every time Daniel broached the subject of finding a new training venue, he preferred to find a way for us to stay in Paris. Finally, one of Daniel's former students, one of the greatest French fencers of all time, Philippe Boisse, offered his club in the Parisian suburbs: Saint Gratien. It was a stunning fencing hall with natural lighting, lots of memorabilia on the walls and, best of all, it was located only 20 minutes away from my apartment.

This camp was even more multinational than the one in Switzerland. Here we had the same gang as before, but requests had come in from the Greek women's team, a Dutch girl, a New Zealand girl and a Moroccan guy. Daniel approved all of them and we had all Olympic zones covered at one training camp. Bring in a few cameras and we could have held the Games there!

Training was shorter during the day, but the camp seemed longer as we crept closer and closer to the big day. Not one to change an effective workout, Daniel had us do the same core body-strengthening exercises everyday. Near the end of the camp Julie looked down at her chest as she was getting out of the shower: "I can't tell which are my boobs and which are my abs!" she said. Ab development is the bane of my existence, so I said, dripping with sarcasm, "Oh, poor little six-pack girl ... isn't life hard for you!" but as I looked down I realized that for the first time in my life, my ab muscles were quite developed too. Our bodies were ready and now we just needed to get to the last of the three preparatory training camps.

In the last 10 days leading up to the Olympics, the theme was supposed to be rest and relaxation. Daniel had found a location in the south of France and close to the Mediterranean, conveniently hosted by one of his best friends. The climate was exactly the same as that in Athens and we were sure to be treated like gold. Unfortunately for our Olympic preparation, there was a cold spell in Perpignan that lasted the duration of our camp. We all did the Jane Fonda-style calisthenic exercises that Daniel led every morning at 7:00 a.m., burning more calories from shivering than from the jumping jacks.

Every minute of the day was scheduled, right down to our team meetings where we analyzed maps of the Athens Olympic Village and venues with the same intensity of a *Mission: Impossible* team. "Okay, the small cafeteria is only open until 22:00 hours, so if we arrive on the second last bus from the venue we will have missed the food service and will have to complete our daily caloric intake in the large cafeteria. Roger that?"

When we had memorized the layout of the Olympic Village, we moved into team analysis, where we reviewed video of our past team matches with Hungary. At the time, I found it completely depressing as they beat us by a huge score every single time, but in retrospect, I know it is necessary to analyze your opponent and replay their actions in your head so that when you see them in front of you there are no surprises and faster reactions.

The hosts of that camp were wonderfully kind and generous and the food was as good as you would expect in the south of France. All this made it reasonably enjoyable. For a rest day, Daniel had scheduled an afternoon of sea kayaking, which was a brand-new experience for nearly everyone. I had never considered how unbalanced fencers are in terms of upper and lower body strength until I saw Jean-Claire, our kayak instructor. His upper body was bulky and full of rippling muscles while his two thighs together would have measured less than any one of ours. Unlike fencing, sea kayaking is not dependent on leg and glute strength, so we were destined to be failures on the open water. I think Jean-Claire knew that and he took it slow with us. We had a nice few hours paddling around the jagged, rocky coast and even did some snorkelling, which, after experiencing even 10 seconds of snorkelling in Cuba, is disappointing anywhere else. Finally, near the end of our sojourn, he threw us a bone. "Who wants to try Eskimotage?" We all looked confused. The Europeans started pointing at us, "You're Canadian, you have Eskimos!"

Jean-Claire waited patiently to explain the process, but after "You purposely roll into the water …" I stopped listening. I had not stopped shivering since our plane landed. Plus, I am a Prairie girl. For me the "open water" is the irrigation canal in the month of June. To Jean-Claire's delight, there were some in the group who were willing to try. Sophie gave it a whirl and ended up almost succeeding in rolling her submerged kayak upright. When Silvio saw that a girl had tried and practically succeeded, he knew he had to do it. So down he went. And up he came. After only a few tries he had successfully performed an "Eskimotage" and only *slightly* injured his fencing arm!

Jean-Claire was very proud of the brave Eskimotagers and he explained that normally this exercise is done while paddling at full speed because you hardly ever fall over from a static position. When Silvio stands up, he measures more than six foot two and looks well older than his twenty-four years. But here, seated low in his kayak with his bulky lifejacket pushed up around his ears and his wet hair plastered to his forehead like a South American monk, he looked about 12. With a big, goofy grin on his face he started paddling directly toward us gaining speed and rapidly closing the distance with each stroke. About two metres before contact, he stopped paddling, stretched his smile even bigger and plunged sideways into the water. Our little show-off Venezuelan was determined to Eskimotage at full speed like the pros. Silvio seemed so full of confidence and athletic ability that we confidently waited for him to pop up. We waited.

And we waited.

After about 15 seconds with his boat still overturned and not a ripple on the water we realized that maybe he *wasn't* going to do it. He was going to die a victim of his own ego. I felt like I was in one of my dreams where there is something terrible happening and no one does anything about it and I am left screaming for help but no words come out. I looked around and sure enough, no one seemed to be doing anything about Silvio's underwater adventure. So I screamed. And this time words came out. "Jean-Claire, Jean-Claire! Help Silvio! Help him!" I was yelling so loud that Jean-Claire looked up almost irritated. I pointed to where Silvio was still submerged and Jean-Claire's eyes grew wide. He paddled over to where Silvio was just starting to pop up, no longer wearing a smile. After that episode Jean-Claire announced our day had come to a close and we went back to the hotel with the image of Silvio's eager grin before his life-threatening Eskimotage.

At the end of the 10 days when we left the camp we wondered why we felt mentally fatigued and more than just a little worn-down physically. When we had showed up at "Les Palmiers," which was the resort where we would spend most of our non-sleeping time, we saw with a disappointing sigh that it was a family resort. There were more children here than at a McDonald's Playland, and while they were relatively well behaved they were still … everywhere.

From my gynecologist to my mother-in-law to the sports writer for the *Ottawa Sun*, everyone is always asking when am I going to have a baby. Sure, I am "of age" and I do have a husband who would make a better father than Mike Brady, but to be honest, I can barely take care of myself at this point, much less a dependent child. Our goldfish keep me stressed out enough, "Are they sick? Why are they swimming so fast? Is the water quality good enough? Am I doing a good job?" I can't even imagine asking similar questions about a child! Plus, being pregnant is a real bother when you are trying to zip up your fencing jacket.

Unless I want to be the travelling circus parent who takes my kid on the road, I have to wait until my sports career is done to have children. Silvio told us once how a media person had asked him where his home address was. Without a moment's hesitation he answered, "Air France, Seat 36F." It took a second to sink in, but we all agreed with a sad laugh that in the year before the Olympics we'd have a better chance of picking up our mail if it was put on our airplane seat than if it were sent to our homes.

The Olympics. Arrival
August 11–31, 2004

Here we were on yet another airplane. We didn't lose heart for two reasons: it was practically the last flight of the season and *we were on our way to the Olympics*! However, feeling completely at home on this tiny plane from Perpignan to Paris was impossible because there were only about 20 rows and each of them with 2 seats, so Silvio's 36F was nowhere to be found. Even though Athens was within cycling distance (as proved by my husband and father-in-law, who were cycling from Paris to Athens and were only a day away by now), there were no direct flights from our training camp to Athens, so we left our hotel at 5:15 a.m., flew to Paris, and then flew down to Athens, arriving there in the early evening. Our flight from Paris to Athens was sure to be run by an efficiently unfriendly Air France crew who lived in the efficiently unfriendly city of Paris, but the crew from Perpignan were clearly country mice: friendly and energetic. You can always tell who is used to working the morning shift because the time of day has no affect on their enthusiasm level.

"Bon-jour!" the flight attendant sing-songed, and with her fire-engine red fingernails took my boarding pass.

"YES!" she exclaimed as I entered the only aisle in the tiny airbus 318. "It is straight down this aisle! Good!" (As though I were in danger of turning the other way and heading into the cockpit.) "Just keep going, madame, and you will see row 17 located after a few other rows!"

I thought to myself with a smirk, "Like after 16 of them?" and thanked her very much as I walked away.

Out popped another eager flight attendant, "Hello, Miss! Can I help you find your way to your seat?" At a loss for words, I just looked at him and like most continually patronized people I actually started to second-guess myself. Maybe I did need help to move from where I was now in row 14 to find this seemingly elusive row 17. "Yeah, help would be nice," I resigned and he ushered me to my seat.

Catherine and I were the first to make the national team in March 2004 (on points earned at pre-selected competitions on the World Cup scene). The next two were selected by the coach in May 2004, and he chose Monique and Julie. Unfortunately for us all, Marie-Eve didn't make the team, but as part of the national team in 2003, she had helped us win the team berth. Although she has since "retired," I am sure she will have a great influence on Canadian fencing in the future because she is doing some coaching now. Our only regret is that "Mama M'eve" could not be there with us to experience the Big Show.

The flight to the Olympics was with Olympic Airways, whose symbol is a mad concoction of rings. When the flight attendants came around to serve drinks, the man next to me ordered a beer. Along the rim of the beer can I saw the words "Official Sponsor of Olympic." A beer company was one of the official sponsors? I guess if McDonald's could do it, so could a beer company, but it was shocking nonetheless. At least McDonald's serves salads. What healthy option could a beer company offer? How could an official sponsor also be on the official banned substance list? As my neighbour put his can down on his tray table, I saw that I had not read the whole motto. What it actually said was, "Official Sponsor of Olympic Airways." The commercialism of the Games had already begun and we weren't even in Athens yet.

When we did arrive, there was a crush of activity. People, luggage, accreditation, buses, media, chaos. Forget commercialism, this was the Olympics that I remembered from Sydney. Everything happening at once and people just going with the flow. There was something different this time, though. No one was there to meet us. Usually there are Canadian staff members there ready to greet us and show us where to put our luggage for transfer to the Village and give us a cold drink or something. This time there was no one, so we just sort of waited for our luggage to come out while we mulled over what to do. As we were standing by the baggage carousel, a guy came and stood beside us. "Are you Canadian?" he asked.

"Yeah, we're here for the Olympics."

"To compete?"

"Yes. In fencing."

"Where are you all from?"

We went through the list of Montreal, London, Brooks ... and Calgary.

"Wow, I'm from Calgary!" he said taken aback.

Imagine the irony of the first person we meet at the Olympics being from one of our home cities. He and Catherine started talking about where exactly they lived in the city, their favourite restaurants, et cetera, and when they started mentioning which schools they went to, my ears perked up.

"Did you say Strathcona Tweedsmuir?" I asked our new friend.

After he nodded I asked him, "Was Bill Jones your principal?"

"Yeah, he was!" he looked shocked so I explained, "I'm from Brooks, Alberta, and Bill Jones was our band teacher before he moved to Strathcona Tweedsmuir to run your school." From weird to weirder.

We finally grabbed our luggage, bid farewell to our new friend and headed toward the exit sign where the rest of the athletes, media and spectators were streaming. With our huge, official red and white fencing bags we made quite a scene and the cameras were all over us. None of us was used to this kind of attention so we tried our very best to look natural, but I couldn't help laughing when Monique leaned over and said, "Now you know how Jessica Simpson feels!" Once outside, it was pretty obvious where we caught the buses so we just threw our bags in a huge truck like everyone else and piled onto a bus. By a stroke of luck I was seated near one of my favourite athletes of all time, Giovanna Trillini, a foil fencer. She is—besides being a four-time Olympic gold medallist— a park ranger in Italy. It was nice to catch up again, and I always smile at how different it must be for her to have to bust poachers in the Italian forest reserve when she is so gentle in everyday life.

We arrived at the Village in time for supper and bed because the next morning began with a wake-up call at 7:00 a.m. We had training, and although the venue wasn't too far, Daniel wanted us awake at the same time we would have to get up the morning of our event, so 7:00 it was! We walked over to the training venue which was past a small security gate, through a pine forest, around a swimming pool and located under the bleachers of the outdoor track. Under the bleachers. Not in the bleachers because they were too full of people watching the track athletes train. We were relegated to under the bleachers.

After training we had a meeting with the RCMP. You probably remember hearing all the possible threats to security at the Athens Olympics: supposedly the Olympic stadium was only a short trip away from the "hot" terrorist areas. To ease the minds of the athletes, their federations and the world at large, the Athens Olympic Committee spent over four billion dollars on security. Canada took its own security measures, bringing along an RCMP officer to work hand-in-hand with local and national policing units to guarantee our safety. Our meeting today was with this officer. "Hello," he began, "would you like the talk in English or French?" We looked at Daniel, who had felt lost since he arrived with Team Canada and had realized that we really are a country that speaks two languages, one of which he did not understand at all. "French," we decided. "Okay, so I am here as your liaison with the security. I have personally seen local security measures and let me assure you that they are amazing. When it comes to security, you have absolutely no need for concern.

Everything is perfectly run and there are no holes in the system. It is airtight."

He spoke with such confidence that I almost believed him. I looked around at my teammates and they were all trying to repress their laughter because in spite of the amazingly "airtight" security, we had managed to sneak Julie in on an invalid pass. She was the alternate for the team, but she did not have permission to stay in the Village. While Team Canada worked tirelessly to get her daily passes, there were still times when, unbeknownst to them, we had to get her into the Village or into the training venue illegally (we really didn't think it was a serious breach of the rules), and we had no trouble doing it. I don't know, perhaps the money they put into security went into behind the scenes work that no one would ever appreciate, because security *was* effective, and there were no problems to point at.

On our first full day in the Athletes' Village we were given an orientation session from the Canadian Olympic Committee staff. They showed us around the Canadian turf and told us about the many services that were offered. Claire Carver-Dias, Michael Smith and Helene Bourdages were the amazing Athletes' Services staff that we interacted with on a day-to-day basis, as they were based in the Athletes' Lounge. Claire began the orientation, "So, we are sitting in the Athletes' Lounge. It is reserved strictly for athletes."

"How strictly reserved? Can the coaches come in here and hang out as well?" Since we were sharing an apartment with our coach and team manager, we were eager to find a place where we could be more or less alone. When I told my training partner Zahra Gamir that we were all men and women in the same apartment, she was shocked. "Like the same building?" she asked.

"No, the same apartment. We share a toilet with the coach."

She gasped, "Oh no, no, no, no. That is not good, that would *never* happen with my team!"

Zahra is from Algeria, and is a very strict Muslim. Usually we are shocked at how rigid gender segregation is in her culture, but after finding out that we had to share an apartment with the smelly guys, I rethought the advantages of this way of life.

After orientation we went to check out the medical / physio / massage rooms to see how soon we could get spoiled. I made an appointment for later that day and when I returned, one of the massage therapists saw me talking with someone he knew. "Hi," he introduced himself, "I'm sorry I don't know you yet; are you one of the coaches or team managers?" I was honestly shocked. Did I no longer look 18? Had I gotten so wrinkled and soft that I could only be a coach or manager? I didn't have the courage to ask and when I explained that I was actually an athlete he went beet red.

The judgements that are made about people according to their body shape or development are even more pronounced in an Olympic Village than in everyday life. You would never walk up to someone with a big belly and say, "Hmmm, now since you have the shape of someone who does a lot of sitting I am guessing you work as a ... truck driver. Am I right?" But all's fair in the closed circle of Olympic sport. In the cafeteria, the games room or the bus, we were both victims and perpetrators of this cycle. "Hey, Monique, did you see that guy's skinny legs? For sure he's a long-distance runner. And what about that group of tiny girls with square shoulders eating honey packets. Are they gymnasts or what!" Some athletes' sports were easier to identify than others. Swimming was pretty much a dead giveaway, especially if it was Ian Thorpe walking by. But there were other sports that were less easy to pinpoint. Who can tell an equestrian from a pentathlete? Asking other people to guess our sport by looking at our body shapes was always worth a laugh. I received a lot of "rhythmic gymnastics." I guess I look too tall and old to be an artistic gymnast, but I definitely don't have the musculature of a track athlete or a swimmer.

Going to the on-site gym was an experience I will treasure forever. You would imagine that in a gym full of Olympians everyone would be strutting their stuff. It would be like going to Venice Beach with Fabio and Madonna. Well, you couldn't be more wrong. The gym in the Athletes' Village was one of the nicest places I have ever worked out! Normally in the gym atmosphere, something comes over some men and they feel that it is their universal duty to correct the technique, posture and general conduct of any female they find. And worse, they will use this mentoring act as an excuse to make physical contact. So we develop automatic responses like, "Thanks, but no thanks" or "Get lost, creep" or we just wear our Walkmans and pretend not to hear. But in Olympic-land there was none of this behaviour. I have spent many hours wondering why no men dared to give out their usual dose of unsolicited advice and I have developed three theories. The men don't dare say anything because the women look so tough. Even the Mexican girls in their bright, pink national uniforms gave you the don't-even-talk-to-me impression of self-assurance. The second reason is an extension of the first: perhaps the men couldn't tell who the women were with testosterone and aggression levels being pretty equal among everyone there. My final theory is my strongest and is probably the real reason why the men left the women alone and the women equally ignored the men at the Olympic gym: athletes are completely self-obsessed. This is true to such an extent that they don't even notice other people when they workout. Were I to be married to someone entirely self-obsessed, I would probably go completely mad, but in a gym setting it is quite refreshing.

After our first few days of training, but before our competition day, comes Opening Ceremonies. This is the one Olympic event huge enough to make even non-sports fans take hours out of their busy schedules surfing the net, or reading Patricia Cornwell's newest book, and instead turn on the television and watch raptly. Everyone watches for something different. Some people watch to see what outfits the different countries are wearing, some watch for famous people. Still others watch the performances, and the rest just hang on to catch the fireworks at the end. To be a part of that excitement is a once in a lifetime opportunity. Okay, maybe it is a twice in a lifetime opportunity, because I had the chance to go in Sydney as well. I had regretted declining to attend the Ceremonies in Sydney and I had every intention of attending them in Athens. There was one day of rest between the Ceremonies and the individual competition, so I was certain that I would have time to recover. What I did not take into account, however, was that with all the training camps, travel, media relations and pre-Olympic hype, I would be completely exhausted even before the Opening Ceremonies. Knowing that what I had spent the last four years training for was coming up in two short days, I didn't feel like wearing myself out needlessly. While I have a clear social side to my personality, I cherish my alone time, and leading up to the Olympics, that alone time was difficult to come by. I honestly didn't think I could handle a stadium of screaming fans for hours on end, so I told myself that being a part of this worldwide excitement was a *thrice* in a lifetime opportunity and I would have to catch the Opening Ceremonies in Beijing 2008.

This evening called for a little otherworldly drama so I went to my room, turned on my computer and popped in my DVD of *Return of the King*. Just as Aragorn was riding into the mountain of death to seek out a ghostly army I heard the computerized strains of "O Canada." Each Canadian athlete had been given a cell phone with eight hundred minutes of talking time for the duration of the Olympics. Every cell phone was programed to ring with our national anthem so that even if you happened to be on the bus sitting among the Japanese team you would know the phone was for you.

"... our home and native land ..." I picked it up.

"Hey, Sheppy!" It was my brother Sherwin calling from Calgary. "I am taping the Opening Ceremonies on CBC but I can't see you anywhere!"

"Uh, yeah, that's because the CBC doesn't have a live feed of my bedroom."

"What?! You didn't go? Oh, bummer. Hey, there's Monique! Well, I taped it for you so you can watch it at Christmas."

"Great, thanks! Well I better go now; things are heating up in Middle Earth."

"Hey, good luck in a few days. You know we're always proud of you, right?"

I knew. If I have ever seen a family as supportive as mine, I don't remember when.

Most of my family had all arrived safe and sound in Athens. This included my husband, my parents, my sister, her husband and their two children, my mother- and father-in-law, and my sister-in-law. It was quite a tight squeeze into the Greek coach's apartment, but they managed it with thankful enthusiasm. Even though my family was in town, Daniel's orders were to stay in the Village for the days leading up to our event, so I spent a lot of time on the phone. The biggest day of my competitive career was approaching and I was starting to get nervous.

I had been to the Olympics before. I was much less tired this time: the flight to Athens was nothing compared to the flight to Sydney. I felt much less intimidated than in 2000. I knew from experience that everything would be taken care of and all we had to do was focus on our event. Experience teaches a lot, and I wasn't going to be such a deer in the headlights when the vast scale of the event washed over me. In fact, on the bus ride from the airport to the Olympic Village when I sat with one of my fencing heroes, Giovanna Trillini, I wasn't even shy about sitting next to someone who had won everything there is to win in fencing. She was just one of the many international friends I had made in sport. Perhaps that alone best marks the change in my attitude.

I have a friend who is in the United States Army and he had one question for me: "How does someone manage to sleep the night before her Olympic event?" I guess I could have asked him how he sleeps before a dangerous mission. Being asked this question almost seemed to pull me out of my life and heady circumstances—it made it all seem less real at that moment. It also made me aware of the fact that, actually, I was extremely nervous.

The Olympics: Competition

have heard all the lines about nerves: "Being nervous means you are ready. Being nervous shows you care. Being nervous is normal." Forget ready and normal, I just wanted to win. I was definitely in the best shape of my life. I had worked a lot tactically, technically and physically. The only thing I was lacking (which barely a handful of other girls have in the whole world) was mental preparation and emotional control. This is something that women athletes especially need to have because we can't seem to channel our negative emotions into that aggressive energy the way male athletes readily can.

I had been preparing myself to concentrate on the fencing but I had not actually replaced the fearful thoughts in my mind with anything else. Before starting my match, my mind was like a wild horse I was trying to rein in, and it proved too difficult. The sudden panic hit me with a shock. My warm-up had been fabulous. I felt limber, fast and observant. Had I gone directly from the warm-up room to the stadium, I can assure you that I would have fenced more like myself. However, each athlete was ushered into a quiet room, seated beside their opponent and told to wait for the televisions to be cued up, at which point we were marched out to their piste under glaring lights and in front of screaming fans.

As I started my match I realized that I was not experiencing that numb awareness that is so crucial to my performance. I was hyper-aware and affected by everything around me. Time seemed to go too fast, and yet at the same time things happened painfully slow as I watched my sporting nightmare unfold. My opponent was Gianna Christou, a Greek fencer I had defeated in Göteborg only this past January. However, it seemed that this time our roles would be reversed. Spurred on by the shouts of "Hellas! Hellas!" coming from the crowd, she moved ahead in the score. She was only up by one or two points at any particular time, but it felt like an enormous lead as I frantically looked to my coach for instruction. He calmly told me to keep a bigger distance but every-thing seemed exaggerated and I already felt too far away to hit her. The match was suddenly finished and a feeling of disbelief came over me. Did I really just lose? Is it really over? Can't I have just one more chance? I had lost 15–13.

Fencing is a cruel sport: nine-minute matches of single elimi-nation. At least tennis players get to play for longer than the time it takes to cook oatmeal. If you are "on," fencing is an incredibly generous sport because you only have to withstand nine minutes of desperate attacks from your opponent and only five short matches before you are crowned the winner. If you are off your game, however, nine minutes does not seem long enough to process a tactical thought much less implement any sort of game plan and try to rally. It is truly a sport of fast thinking and mental discipline like no other. These are the reasons why I love it and hate it.

Stunned, I waited as the volunteers came over to escort me back to the warm-up room. Only then did I look into the crowd where my family was seated. The stands were not very well lit but I thought I caught sight of my five-year-old nephew, Ethan, standing up, his arm outstretched, giving me a thumbs-up. My sister told me later that in the middle of my match when Ethan

saw that I was losing, he stood up and shouted with the simple bril-
liance of a five-year-old, "You just have to go *faster*, Auntie Shep!"
When he saw that I lost anyway, he said he was still proud of me,
and that's when he stood up to give me the one-thumb salute. I
guess this is why two-thirds of the women's épée medal winners
over the last two Olympics have been mothers. Having children
makes you tougher and parenthood allows you to appreciate what
is important, letting you relax enough to perform at your best.

Even though my individual Olympic competition was done for at
least the next four years, the worst was yet to come. After leaving
the venue, I was shepherded past a penned-in crowd of journalists.
In the past few years I have met some absolutely wonderful people
who work in and with the media. Some of them have become dear
friends who truly want the best for me and are respectful and
compassionate. In the mood I was in, I didn't see too many of those
people as I trudged past the media scrum. They were leaning out
on tiptoe from behind the metal barriers, pencils wagging and tape
recorders rolling, asking the most inane of all questions:
"Sherraine, how do you feel?"

Honestly, now how am I supposed to respond to that? Let's
see, my 17 years of fencing have all been dedicated to succeeding
at this moment, and now it was over before I could say "en guard."
Do they really want to know how I *feel* or do they want to know
how I plan to deal with those feelings? Because the way I feel is
pretty nasty. I feel absolutely beat-up, embarrassed, shocked,
exhausted, angry, and frustrated—and the depression hasn't even
set in yet. How would these journalists react if I came running up
to them as they were walking away from their boss's office having
just been fired? Imagine they had handed in their most passion-
ately written and researched piece and their boss had discarded it?
"How do you feel?" I would ask. "You have just given it your all but
you've come up short? What are you *feeling* right now?"

Sherraine MacKay

In the Olympic Qualification year before the 2000 Sydney Olympics I had seven consecutive tournaments where I finished 33rd. Whenever I would call to report my results to my mother, she would reassure me in that maternally encouraging way, "Well, dear, at least this year you are very consistently in the round of 64, so you can be proud of that!" Mom was obviously not aware that since I was ranked in the top 16 in the world, all I had to do was *register* for the competition and I automatically qualified for the first elimination round of 64. Bless her heart for trying to encourage me in my darkest moments. Wow, could I ever have used a serving of that right then.

Honestly, after my big loss, the only person I wanted to see was my husband. I walked out into the crowd and looked for him but he, too, was being occupied by the press. What sort of circus had my life become in the past 10 minutes? I was thankful that fencing was a fairly low-profile sport because I wouldn't want to deal with this on an everyday basis. When we finally saw each other, there were many hugs and a few tears as we alone understood how hard the journey was and how quickly it was now over. There were no platitudes of "I'm proud of you. You did your best. Hey, at least you made it to the Olympics." While all those things are true, they did not need to be said at that moment. So he held me and we just stayed quiet and still while the gym around us was buzzing with excitement.

I asked the media to give me some time as I went to the warm-up room with my coach. Although brief, we had a pretty open talk where I was able to express things that had been bothering me over the past few months. Then I was ready to meet the press. Trying to relay my sense of disappointment was practically impossible, but I tried, and with the exception of one extremely obtuse woman who worked for the Canadian French-speaking media and who told me, "So, Sherraine, you really did all the things you said you wouldn't and you didn't do any of the things you said you would ...," the journalists were quite respectful, at least at that moment.

After that, the CBC wanted to speak with me so my family

came along to check out the studio. It wasn't a big deal for Jeff; being a hockey player he had seen many television studios, but for the rest of my family it was pretty cool. We got to meet Brian Williams, Ron MacLean, Catriona Le May Doan, Mark Tewksbury, and I finally met, in person, Robin Brown! Robin and I had become friends when she interviewed me for her CBC Radio One show *The Inside Track*. A wonderfully kind person, she is also a great journalist, and seeing the face behind the voice was one of the highlights of my Olympics.

The rest of the day passed in sort of a haze. The rest of the Canadian girls were disappointed, losing their matches in the first round or the second like I had. Monique won her first bout in the round of 64 against Rachel Barlow of South Africa only to lose in her next match with China's Li Na. Catherine lost her first bout in the round of 64 against Eimey Gomez of Cuba. I watched the remaining matches, went for lunch with my family and then came back for the finals. In the end it was back-to-back Olympic gold medals for Timea Nagy of Hungary who defeated Laura Flessel-Colovic of France for the gold.

I think that everyone has those heightened emotions that surround disappointment. It is how we deal with those emotions that's interesting. They are best dealt with upfront and immediately. First of all, you have to admit they are there. Because I am a Christian, people often think that the only appropriate reaction is to plaster a big grin on my face. But we all know there is no sense in smiling through the pain when it becomes a false optimism. One of the biggest mistakes people make as Christians is thinking that they have to be happy all the time. I remember singing a song in Sunday school, "I'm in right, outright, upright, downright happy all the time!" Obviously, the songwriter had never stepped out the front door and had certainly never lost in the second round at the Olympics because that statement just can't be true. They've never read the Book of Lamentations or some of David's Psalms in the Bible, either, because expressing your frustration to God is the best way to deal with it. Believe me, there have been many "Why bring me this far just to have me fail?" conversations since that day. I know now that God does not hurt me and doesn't "bring me somewhere just to have me fail." Rather, God has a heart full of emotion as well, and hurts with me when I hurt, so there is no shame in telling Him how much something pains me. There are no guarantees in life and no equation will yield certainty of success or even happiness, but a certainty I can speak of is God's goodness and His compassion. One of my favourite quotes is from C. S. Lewis' children's classic *The Lion, the Witch and the Wardrobe*. Aslan, the character that represents God in the book, is being described to the children, and one of the little girls asks, "Is he safe?" The response is amazing: "No, he's not safe. But he's good." At times of disappointment, when I don't know why things happen the way they do, this is a comforting truth. I know that the one whom I trust is good, and that's more than enough to get me through the difficult times I have had in my life so far.

And let's face it, sports are entertainment. At their best—and ideally—sports reflect universal human ideals. A beautiful body in controlled motion is not a common thing, and it should prompt us to excel even in the daily tasks of our lives. Skill in sport should inspire the mind to develop mental and moral skills. As the athlete reaches for more than what she is physically capable of at a given moment, we are reminded to ask questions in life that take our understanding beyond the pale of the merely physical. But these ideal experiences of athletes and of those who really appreciate athletics are not common; sports are generally entertainment. It's just a game, after all.

One of the hard things about losing was feeling slightly responsible for the downswing in Team Canada's momentum. Instead of waiting excitedly to see how the athletes had done, the print media people seemed to be waiting anxiously for us to keep under-performing. (Christie Blatchford was an exception; she had only good things to say about the athletes' performances and was critical of her colleagues who couldn't see worth in anything besides medals.) Athletes in the Village couldn't help being affected by their harsh criticism. When I read a scathing article about how Nicolas Gill had "fallen short" of his potential like so many other Canadian athletes, my heart went out to him. If any athlete understands how unforgiving a system of elimination can be it is a judoist. Judo is ruthless, and Nicolas Gill is a real champion, who deals with the pressure and has earned two Olympic medals, one in Barcelona, one in Sydney. Athens was an unfortunate exception for him and he underperformed in his first match, losing to someone he normally beats. When I saw him later that night in the cafeteria, I just walked over to him and hugged him. It seems cheesy, but for me, when a high-level athlete loses there is nothing you can say that will help. This may sound morbid or melodramatic, but you just have to treat their loss like a death in the family: don't say too much, and just be compassionate in your actions.

When Nick said to me in a sarcastic, pained laugh, "I followed your example, Sherraine," I knew that my loss affected more than just *my* spirit. Team momentum is an important thing that no one ever talks about. Swimming is traditionally one of France's weakest sports, where they give out medals to people who can just make it across the pool without stopping. My physiotherapist at the Racing Club is a former Olympic swimmer for France and I asked him why he thought the French swimming team had such a great Olympics in Athens. "Momentum," he said. "Someone won early on and the rest of the team got their confidence from that." That is the difference between pressure and confidence. If someone who is not in sport says to you, "You're going to win, right?" it feels like pressure. When your teammate says, "You are going to win, right?" it's confidence. It all comes down to understanding. Outsiders don't and other athletes do. Of course, as athletes—Olympic ones at that—we have to be stronger than what's going on around us. We are by nature able to find confidence in what we are certain is true about ourselves, regardless of what some people may say or how they may treat us. That is why we are the very best at what we do. But it always helps if momentum is on your side ...

Lack of momentum was painfully obvious when we were watching the American basketball team get chewed up and spit out by Argentina in the match to decide who would play for the gold medal. I've never seen such a group of superstars fail so completely to work as a team. The line between amateur and professional athletes was the most obvious with Team USA. The amateurs were star-struck and the professionals just wanted to be left alone. Talking to a couple of Americans, I heard that this led to a lack of unity as well as a lack of team and national pride. I remember the Canadian men's basketball team in Sydney staying in the Village and mixing with the other Team Canada athletes, and several of them were also highly paid NBA superstars, including MVP Steve Nash. The American basketball players, on the other hand, didn't even visit the Athletes' Village in Athens, much less talk to the other athletes, and judging by their style of play, they didn't seem to spend that time practicing together, either. I cannot remember seeing a more disjointed team, and everyone knew it.

We had a day of rest after our individual épée competition before it was training as usual. Our team event was coming up in a few days and we were like ravenous wolves. I felt blessed that unlike the Sydney Olympics, at least I had another chance to fence here.

Running With Swords

None of us had very stellar results individually, so we were extremely motivated to win. Daniel had been repeating the same thing to us since we first qualified by team: "The competition is short and anything can happen … if you win two matches, you'll have a medal around your neck!" Had he gone mad? Our first match was against the number two team in the world: Hungary. Not only were they highly ranked but they had the back-to-back Olympic champion, Timea Nagy, on their team. Our best-ever showing against them was two years ago at the World Cup in Budapest. I was in the last bout with Ildiko Mincza and we were tied. It went into sudden-death overtime. I hesitated and she hit me, winning that match. Every time we have fenced against Hungary we've never even come *close* to beating them.

However, our biggest advantage was that in team competition we really had nothing to lose that day. Nobody expected us to do anything exceptional, least of all the Hungarians, and that was fine by us. We took a small lead of only one or two points but tenaciously held it. On the piste beside us, Greece, the second-last ranked team, jumped into a huge lead against Germany, who were number one overall. The Greeks jumped ahead 8–0 in the first two matches, but by the end the Germans had tied it up and they went into sudden-death overtime.

Christou, the fencer I'd lost to in the individual competition, proved to be less difficult for Imke Duplitzer, who hit her with a lunge for the win.

Back on our piste, things were tense. In the last match, the Hungarians tied it up and I found myself once again in sudden-death overtime with Ildiko Mincza. The next point would decide our Olympic fate. If the Hungarians won and went on to collect a medal, they would all receive lifetime pensions from the government. If we won, we would receive a congratulatory letter from the Canadian Minister of Sport and probably an interview with Ron MacLean. But that was all beside the point. This moment was what amateur sports were made for. All for glory! I didn't have time to think of what had happened in our past matches. I didn't have time to think of what it would be like if we won. I had achieved numb awareness. In my mind's eye, I saw an action that I knew would work. I just felt it. A calm, decisive bravery washed over my body and when we got en guard I knew the point would be mine.

"Allez!" the judge commanded.

We went.

After some back and forth, I pushed her back along the piste to her end. Ildiko is very dangerous when her opponent attacks from up high. She can see them coming and is almost guaranteed to take them low. So I went low. So low that I hit her foot … and scored.

When I realized that we had just won, I turned around to where my teammates and coach were running toward me in incredulous excitement. I shook Ildiko's hand and inside I wished that I could have conveyed all of the respect I had for her in that handshake. She is not only one of the most intelligent women on the circuit, but she is also the most sportsmanlike and kindest. She finished fourth in the individual event a few days earlier, losing her chance at a medal when she refused to take advantage of Laura Flessel-Colovic falling on the piste in the middle of her action. Instead of hitting Laura when she was down, which probably any other fencer on the circuit would have done, Ildiko stopped and offered her hand to help Laura to her feet. The crowd was immediately behind Ildiko and everyone's heart broke when she lost that match, and later the match for the bronze medal as well.

Earlier in the year at the World Cup in Spain, Ildiko took me aside and talked to me about my fencing. "Sherraine, I don't know for sure but you don't really seem happy with your fencing. Are you still enjoying it? Because it is important to find pleasure in this sport; otherwise, there is not much point in participating. I have been competing for many years and I know that you have to love it to make it worth your while." This was not a ploy on her part to find out my weak points. She just really and truly cared and her only intention was to help me. In truth, I had started to take fencing too seriously, seeing winning or losing as my defining moment. I thought that if I couldn't win, it meant I was not as strong a person as I once thought. The pressure from my coach, from the media, and worst of all, from myself to win everything had become a heavy weight to bear. The pressures increased as Athens approached and every bout in training or in competition seemed indicative of how I would perform at the Olympics. I would get so angry when I wasn't winning. No one can live comfortably for very long under these conditions, and it was pretty obvious that I was at my breaking point.

Also, I believe I was just plain out of steam. My schedule was pretty hectic; I had taken only three weeks off throughout the past three years, and I had travelled all over the world trying to be at my best all the time. Looking back, I should have taken a good break just prior to the Olympics, but it may have been too late by then. I've come to recognize the importance of rest in such a cerebral sport.

I remember Ildiko telling me that you can't go around being angry all the time. Sometimes you win and sometimes you don't, but if you never find enjoyment in the sport, what is the point of doing it? We don't get paid enough to do it as a job so we have to find some sort of pleasure and redemption in doing it.

As Tatiana Logounova would say to Geordie later that day when Russia beat us to advance to the gold medal match: "I am sorry, but that is sport." Russia was the next team we had to face and, unfortunately for us, they were not as unsteady as Hungary. None of them had performed exceedingly well in individual, and they were full of desire to win and backed with a healthy dose of discipline from their bear of a coach.

Waiting for Julie and Monique to finish their bouts was a painful process, not because I worried about the score or wanted to do it all myself, but because my elbow on my fencing arm was throbbing like it had been run over by a truck. I had a serious case of tendonitis. Our precious Canadian doctor, Pierre Fremont, had already given me an injection of painkiller a few times earlier that morning. For some reason, be it stress, excitement or old age, the effect of the shot would disappear in a matter of 10 or 15 minutes. I would then be writhing in pain, and something as basic as opening a water bottle was out of the question. So Pierre and I became fast friends, spending all day by each other's side. "Pierre! I can feel my elbow again!" I would say minutes before my match, and he'd come running, tapping his syringe and telling me to roll up my sleeve. Doctors with needles at my disposal, thousands of people watching me compete, every joint in my over-used body failing me—I felt like an NFL player.

We stayed close to them throughout the match, always within one or two points, and when it came to the last bout against Tatiana Logounova, we were tied at only 13-13. Our slow, careful advance throughout the match gave us more room for error at the end, and by the time I got to the final bout, we had three minutes left, or 32 points—whichever came first.

This last bout with Tatiana was very intense and very physical—physical enough for the judge to award one of my points to her instead. Tatiana is known for her brutal fencing, and it was ironic that at that moment I was the one receiving the warning for unnecessary physical contact. Here at the Olympics, our match started off tied and when I unwisely went low on her, she picked off my hand and moved ahead by one touch. Then we exchanged doubles for a while and the score moved up to 17-16 in Russia's favour.

Next came the turning point. Very often I can hit Tatiana with a running attack because she doesn't back up very well in her own territory. I pushed her into her own end, flèched and hit her directly in the chest. I wanted to make sure that I landed the point; the chances to move into the gold medal round at the Olympic Games are pretty rare. As I forced my arm to keep pushing through the action, she stepped in and lifted her bell guard directly into mine. CLANG. Maybe it was the meds, but I didn't even really notice our collision. But the judge did, and to prove that he was not letting any roughhousing happen on his piste, thank you very much, he annulled my hit. It was a clean hit but he didn't see it that way. He thought I was using "brutality" so he also awarded me a yellow card, meaning the next time something like that happened, she would get a point. While the score would have been tied if he had awarded me my point for my flèche, Tatiana was still ahead by one. The judge's blatant error really contributed to the outcome of the match. There was another collision, and this time Tatiana was awarded a point. Now I really felt like an NHL player, taking penalty after penalty. After that the match drifted away on me as I was always trying to play catch-up. She won 25–18, five of her points scored in the last 10 seconds of the match. It was yet another crushing Olympic moment, the only consolation being that we had another match in a few hours on the final piste where we would take on the French for the bronze medal.

The French were our nemesis. As many times as Hungary had destroyed us, at least we could remind ourselves of that time two years ago where we had been within one point of beating them. We had *never* been that close with France. We had actually beaten or come within one point of beating every other team at the Olympics—except China, who we had never fenced. The French team's style was very difficult for us, but considering our well-fought and unexpected win against Hungary, the sky was the limit! We took a break for a few hours, spending some time with friends and family who had come to watch, and then we warmed up for our match.

The most difficult thing for me about fencing under bright lights in front of thousands of spectators and dozens of cameras was not maintaining concentration or being able to relax, but rather finding a private place before my match to get injected with my new best friend, liquid painkiller. We went to the end of the piste, but as soon as I rolled up my sleeve and Pierre pulled out his needle there were two French cameras on us. The last thing I needed was to have French television showing footage of me getting pumped full of who-knows-what before I beat their team to a pulp. We moved to a corner as far away as possible and I turned my back to their lenses as Pierre went to work. They soon became bored and went back to filming the match.

Having the match televised helped more than I ever imagined. There was a jumbo screen located behind the French team, which meant that during the match we could see the instant, slow-motion replays of all the points. I had never dreamed that this could be so helpful! I could watch the replay to confirm how my opponent had hit me, helping me prepare for the next time they tried to pull out that little number. It was an amazingly efficient corrective device. Likewise, if I scored a point I could revel in the replay, seeing how beautiful and effective it was, giving me even more confidence to try the action again. Good athletes learn whenever and however they can.

Our match with the French team—Maureen Nisima, Hajnalka Kiraly-Picot, and Laura Flessel-Colovic—started out a bit slowly. We had decided that a conservative approach would be the best, keeping the score low and hopefully manageable. Monique started out for Team Canada, fencing against Nisima. We went a bit off the game plan as the score was quickly 4-1 in their favour. Then I had a match with Kiraly-Picot and we were within reach at 6-4, with France still in the lead. Unfortunately Julie's match with Flessel widened the gap a little. We knew we had to get more aggressive. By the time Moe had scored a touch on Kiraly-Picot, we were down 13-4. Frustration began showing as Monique contested one of Kiraly's points, thinking that she had been past before Kiraly had twisted around to make the touch (you can't hit someone once they are no longer in front of you). The judge, however, stuck with his original ruling. We were down 16-7 and time was ticking.

The French were coming on strong by that time. It was 20-8 when I strapped on my sword to take on Flessel-Colovic, who had fenced her way to a silver medal during the individual competition. A lefty, Flessel knows when to use it to her advantage, often making a hit on her opponent's arm or shoulder when she comes in for an attack. I knew we had to step it up, and went in with all guns blazing. I made several points very quickly, starting to feel a momentum growing. Well, this was the time for it! It became a little fast and furious, and Flessel ended up with an injury to her "off hand" (the hand that is not holding an épée, which is also ungloved and therefore easy to injure). She stormed back a bit and we were moving all over the piste in what was by far the most energetic bout of the match. We ended the bout at 30–19. I had made 11 hits but it still hadn't been enough: she countered back with 10 of her own. In the next bout, Julie brought us up within 7 points in a very strong bout against Kiraly-Picot, and at 31-24 it was Monique's turn against Flessel-Colovic. A bunch of double hits later (when two fencers hit each other simultaneously) we were still down 40–31.

It was now-or-never time as I stepped up on the piste to face Nisima in the final bout. I had three minutes to make 10 points, all without letting Nisima make a single one. All she had to do was make five, and the French would get the bronze. After one double hit, I was off to a bad start. Suddenly Nisima lunged at me, and I scored a stop hit by hitting her arm as it came at me. Overbalanced, she came down hard on her right leg. Hopping up, she continued the match, and in fact seemed to become even more aggressive, matching me attack for attack. It made sense—the best defence is usually a good offence—and she had to know that I was going to come out hard to try and catch up. The tactic didn't serve her well, however; in the next action she parried my épée down and it slid down her shin. I guess the final straw for her was when she stumbled again on a flèche attack. It was obvious that she was favouring her leg, but that was hard to do when a lunge or a flèche depends on that lead leg as a brake! It was over for Nisima as the French called in their alternate, Sarah Daninthe. Nisima had kept the score to 43–35.

As I waited for Daninthe to prepare, I tried to keep focused, although with this turn of events several things crossed my mind: would Daninthe be properly warmed up, and could I take advantage of this? Would a change in opponents be to my advantage? And with the scoreboard blazing both the score and the time remaining at me, would I have enough in me to make up at least 8 points in 1 minute and 55 seconds?

Finally ready, she came in knowing that she had only to make two points to get the win and that her participation would guarantee that she would be rewarded with a medal (only people who actually take part in the matches receive medals). And after scoring two of my own points, she finally did the same and the French won the bronze. Although we had had an amazing day and had attained our highest ever international result—fourth—our Olympic run was at an end.

There were two moments of consolation, however. Russia absolutely beat up on Germany, and we found some solace in knowing that Canada was by far the toughest match for the back-to-back Olympic champion Russian team. My own personal moment of consolation came when the doping officers approached our team and said that one of us had been randomly chosen to be tested. "Oh, no," I thought. "There goes my whole evening. I am going to be stuck for hours in a small room with a very serious doctor and some person watching me pee … and I thought losing to the French was annoying!" But the officers looked down at their clipboard and said, "Julie Leprechaun?"

"Lep-RO-hon," she corrected, for probably the millionth time in her 25 years of life.

The biggest moment of consolation was that even though we didn't carry home a medal or one of those really cool laurel wreaths the Greek Olympic committee gave to every medallist, we did get far enough in the competition for the CBC to deem fencing worthy to broadcast on television. Live! For at least 45 minutes of Canadian broadcasting, fencing was the spotlight, letting the whole country get a small taste of the excitement and intelligence of this sport. My favourite e-mails after our televised bronze medal match were those that began like this: "I have never watched fencing before and I had no idea it was so thrilling!" Even today when I meet Canadians and they learn that I am a fencer they say, "Oh fencing! I saw some girls doing that on TV... how exciting!" It is phenomenal to be able to say, "Yeah, I was one of those girls!" It is one of my dreams for people to appreciate fencing in Canada and help us become a dominant nation worldwide because I think our national personality fits the sport profile. We are creative and intelligent, competitive but polite, and judging by the amount of people who play hockey, we don't mind putting on excessive amounts of equipment to play a sport. What more do you need to be an accomplished fencer? Oh, yeah—you need a really good yell. So as a nation, let's all start working on our celebratory scream and reconvene in four years' time to pick up where the women's épée team left off. Someday, hopefully sooner than we all think, Canada will be a powerhouse in the world of fencing.

By the time the Closing Ceremonies came around it was completely impossible to identify which country people were from: anyone could be wearing pants from Germany, a sweater from Ecuador, a hat from Nigeria, shoes from Jamaica and an Aussie backpack. Your guess was as good as mine. It actually made it a little complicated to trade at that point. You would ask in very simple English, motioning a trading gesture with your hands, if they wanted to swap clothes. Often you'd get back an apologetic decline: "Sorry, mate, but I just traded for this Tee with a cool bloke from Rio!" Catherine Dunnette and I had a plan to get exactly the clothes we had been eyeing ever since we arrived at the Games. We were going to wait until the last night when everyone was so full of spirits—uh, I mean Olympic spirit—that they would trade their stuff away without caring too much about what was happening. There was one small problem: the Olympic Committee did such a great job planning for the mass exodus of athletes that they had arranged for a Village "luggage check-in." Because of this, most of the athletes had their luggage packed, checked in and sitting at the airport when we got around to trading with them. Finally we struck gold, though. Denmark had beautiful tracksuits and we were anxious to get our hands on one. So at 4:00

a.m., peak party hour for the final night's festivities, we made our way over to Denmark's neighbourhood where the music was pumping and the top floor of their apartment was rocking. We walked into the apartment and we were greeted like old friends. "HEY!" Everyone was yelling and they pulled us into the party room. It was fun and we stayed for a while but we never forgot our purpose. At one point I cornered a Danish girl. "Do you want to change something for your tracksuit?" I asked her.

"Sure!" The exchange was easier than I ever imagined possible and when we began talking about our Olympic experiences, I understood why. "Oh, we get like two or three tracksuits," she said offhandedly. "Denmark's a pretty small team and so they spoil us."

In spite of being Canada's smallest team to qualify in over 20 years, all we were given was one tracksuit per person every four years from Roots. I ended up spending a better part of those wee hours in the morning talking with this Danish athlete. We had a lot in common: we both lived in Europe, worked as teachers, were the youngest in our families and happened to be the captains of our national teams. The only exception was that her team had just won their second straight Olympic title and our team was just starting out. She gave me the quiet inspiration to keep going that only true team captains can give.

That feeling of inspiration had already taken hold during the Closing Ceremonies. The theme was "Looking to Beijing 2008," and that's where I was already headed in my mind's eye. Like anything in life, the Olympics were not so much an achievement as they were a process and journey. My experiences qualifying for and competing in Sydney and Athens had shown me that I can reach beyond what I think is possible and, with that drive still in me, how could I stop?

After Athens, I felt like my training atmosphere had to be fixed somehow. Geordie and I were almost 30 and living like college students. I had a meagre job teaching English. My husband (who had no papers to work legally in France) babysat and gave guitar lessons to earn money. His musical career was improving slowly, but it was nowhere near providing what could be considered a full-time income. We were living in an incredibly small, dingy apartment in a bad area, and I couldn't do this for another four years. As well, life was far from perfect with my coach, Daniel. We both thought that I needed different things. I thought I needed more independence, he thought I needed more direction and instruction. It was time for a change.

My first thought was Budapest. I had always loved the city, it was definitely cheaper than Paris and its athletes always seemed to have a kind of calm independence about them that I admired. I remember watching one fencing master— Gyozo Kulcsar— giving a lesson, and he really pushed his athlete but also had a carefree spirit and genuine enjoyment for fencing. So I phoned his nephew whom I knew from the circuit (Krisztian – my "running partner" at the camp in Hungary), and he set up a meeting when I was travelling through with my parents on our month-long "See Europe" tour just after the Olympics. Kulcsar said he would give me a try and we would see how it went between us. So Geordie and I packed up and moved to Budapest in a rented minivan.

Gone are the days of taking the Metro for hours on end. Now I live around the corner from the fencing centre (the beautiful old synagogue I mentioned)! I don't even stretch or shower at the club; I walk home in 30 seconds and stretch in the comfort of my own living room and shower in my own bathroom. Fencing training at my club is every weekday afternoon for two hours, and two or three mornings per week we have "keret," or group training, where I spar with the whole national team. I do my physical preparation on my own in the mornings. My coach told me that he didn't want to be in charge of that and I was happy to hear that outside of my lessons, I have my longed-for independence! Now I get to experience his lessons, which are unbelievably physical, technical and beautifully tactical but tempered with his blunt encouragement and wacky sense of humour. (During a thunderstorm the other day, when it sounded like the roof was going to come down, Kulcsar pointed at me and said, "God is angry because you are not working hard enough!" and then laughed like crazy.)

When my first fencing coach, Alan Nelson, heard that I was working with this new coach, he got all excited. "Is this the great Kulcsar? Oh, man, I remember seeing him win team gold and individual bronze at the Montreal Olympics in 1976! Good for you to be working with him!" When I meet people in the fencing world they refer to him as "Kulcsar, the Champion." Gyozo Kulscar has won practically everything there is to win in fencing—several times over including individual bronze in 1968 and gold at the 1972 Olympics and he has a few team World Championship titles under his belt, as well. Since retiring from his illustrious career he has coached Olympic and World Champions—but he would never be the one to tell you any of this. That made me think of a conversation I had with him as he waited with me at the doctor's office in Budapest. I had asked my new coach if he had ever been to Canada. He said yes, a long time ago he had once been to Montreal and had enjoyed it very much. In his modesty, he hadn't felt inclined to even mention the Olympic medals he had won there.

So far, it is going very well, except we are even poorer than in Paris because here I have to pay for club fees, gym fees and coaching. These were waived in Paris, thanks to the extremely generous president, Ange Pezzini. With our savings and extremely tight budgeting, we have managed to scrape by, and we hope to be able to do the same for the next four years. Geordie is busy with his music and other odd jobs and we absolutely love the quiet, calm charm of Budapest. It will be a wonderful place to train for the next four years … I hope!

During the Closing Ceremonies in Athens, Nicolas Gill and I had decided to continue our tradition where I sit my 135 pounds on his shoulders and we march into the stadium like an Olympic totem pole. As we walked in, we saw Yao Ming, China's seven-and-a-half-foot tall basketball superstar and I begged Nick to go over so I could see how I measured up with him. When we came close enough, I took the branch of wheat that we had been handed on our way into the stadium and waved it as I stood beside Yao Ming. When he realized there was someone taller than him, he took his wheat stalk and threatened to poke me in the face. Obviously he underestimated his opponent, and we soon had a full-scale fencing match in progress. The Chinese media was snapping photos left and right and eventually Yao submitted to my skill and technique. With the speeches in the background talking about the high hopes for the Beijing Olympics in 2008, I saw Yao Ming's submission in our impromptu sparring match as a foreshadowing to what lay ahead in my life, complete with fiery possibilities and no guarantees.